WEST SUSSEX
EVENTS

Four Centuries of Fortune and Misfortune

The first delivery made by a Foden steam wagon from Constable's Anchor Brewery at Arundel and Littlehampton to the
Murrell Arms, *Barnham behind the last horse-drawn delivery van in 1912. In front are Billy Griffin, Jack Silverlock (killed in the First World War) and Jack Lassiter from Arundel. Wm. Francis Brown, landlord from 1906-19, is in the white hat alongside his son William, landlord from 1929-46, and his daughter Eva. Henry Hall (1835-1915), wheelwright and landlord from 1875-1903, is standing in the doorway, and Charlie Dollery is holding the horse.*

WEST SUSSEX EVENTS

Four Centuries of Fortune and Misfortune

Spencer Thomas

Phillimore

2003

Published by
PHILLIMORE & CO. LTD
Shopwyke Manor Barn, Chichester, West Sussex, England

ISBN 1 86077 261 7

Printed and bound in Great Britain by
BUTLER & TANNER LTD
London and Frome

CONTENTS

LIST OF ILLUSTRATIONS

Frontispiece. The first delivery made by a steam wagon to the *Murrell Arms*, Barnham.

Acknowledgements

The author gratefully acknowledges the contributions of numerous people particularly Richard Childs, County Archivist, for his generosity and support, his staff at the West Sussex Record Office including Susan Millard, Assistant Archivist, who researched the photographs and Claire Snoad who transferred them onto CD-Rom, and the Search Room staff who supplied material promptly with a smile. Above all I am indebted to Kim Leslie for his introduction, guidance, encouragement and generosity in sharing his encyclopaedic knowledge of the sources and content of the local history of West Sussex, and Martin Hayes, Principal Librarian – Local Studies – West Sussex County Council Library Services who, besides researching and providing numerous images, gave me the benefit of his experience and knowledge of local history. Both went beyond the call of duty and will recognise their imprint in these pages, but responsibility for the text and selection of the images rests solely with the author. At Phillimore I am indebted to Simon Thraves (Commissioning Editor) for advice with the contents and text and to Andrew Illes who skilfully married the text and images and to the firm for the supportive environment it offered at every stage.

The bulk of the book is derived from original archival sources but the author gratefully acknowledges his debt to other researchers and authors of books, articles and theses on which he has drawn including Edward Bishop, Barry Fletcher, James Gardner, Martin Hayes, Jeremy Hodgkinson, Kim Leslie, John Lowerson, Ron Iden, E.M. Jones, Hugh Mathews, Alison McCann, Tim McCann, Alan Readman, R.W. Standing, Emlyn Thomas. He is also indebted to everyone who alerted him to possibilities, provided information and/or photographs, gave permission to use material, allowed him into their homes to take photographs and in many other ways: Chichester Festival Theatre, English Bowling Association, Environment Agency, Geological Museum, Imperial War Museum, Portsmouth and Sunderland Newspapers, Queen Victoria Hospital Museum, East Grinstead, Sussex Archaeological Society, WSCC Archives, WSCC Local Studies, Adrianne Blaikie (Richard Lochner's daughter), Geoffrey Collier, Julia Tickner, Lynne Ingram.

The sources of the photographs are as follows: Author, 19, 25, 27, 28, 36, 41, 42, 54, 57, 60, 62, 66, 68, 76, 108, 118, 120, 121, 131, 132; Adrianne Blaikie, 103; David Breffett, 96, 97, 98, 99; Chichester Festival Theatre, 102, 130; Neville Duke, 122; English Bowling Association, 123; Environment Agency, 12; *Evening Argus*, 8; Geological Museum, 1; Joan and Ron Ham, 2, 129; B. J. Hardy, 7; Imperial War Museum, 104; Peter Jerrome, 61; E.W. Jones, 112, 113; Lord Egremont, 67, 81; Kim Leslie, 128; Bob Marchant, 119; Tim McCann, 124; Portsmouth and Sunderland Newspapers, 11, 51, 52, 53; R.W. Standing, 84, 85; Sussex Archaeological Society, 135, 136, 137; University College, Chichester, 24, 26, 29, 56, 59, 92, 93; West Sussex County Council Archives (Record Office), *frontispiece*, 3, 4, 5, 6, 13, 14, 15, 16, 17, 18, 20, 21, 38, 39, 40, 48, 50, 65, 69, 70, 72, 77, 78, 79, 80, 89, 94, 105, 111, 116, 117, 126, 138, 139, 141, 143; West Sussex County Council Library Service (Local Studies), 9, 10, 22, 23, 30, 32, 33, 34, 35, 37, 43, 44, 45, 46, 47, 55, 58, 63, 64, 71, 73, 74, 75, 82, 83, 86, 88, 90, 91, 106, 107, 108, 109, 110, 114, 125, 127, 133, 134, 140, 142.

One

ACTS OF GOD

Quaking with Fear

Acts of God are familiar to most people because they figure in clauses in their insurance policies, but they are usually dismissed with 'it won't happen to me'. In reality they don't just happen to 'someone else' and actuaries know that events in this category can impact upon anyone, hence their incorporation as insurance risks. Even those associated in the popular psyche with 'far away places' can hit nearer home.

Earthquakes have been recorded in West Sussex over the centuries, with graphic descriptions in the *Anglo-Saxon Chronicle* in the 11th century. The first great tremor in 1158 killed three people and caused substantial damage. In 1382 the Bell Tower in Chichester Cathedral was 'shook down' and in 1580 the bell 'strake itselfe against ye hammer with shaking as divers clockes and bells in the city and elsewhere did the like'. A contemporary chronicler commented, 'There was heard a marvelkouse great noyse … and therewith began a most feirc and terrible earthquake'. In 1638 a quake

1 *West Sussex has a long legacy of earthquakes. Massive outcrops of Ardingly Sandstone in Chiddingly Park, referred to as the 'earthquake beds', provide evidence of seismic activity about 120 million years ago.*

1

was accompanied by 'a smell like pitch and sulphur'. In 1734 there were 'tremblings'. In 1750 there were a succession of earthquakes over three months which led the poor to believe 'The End of the World and the Last Judgement were nigh'. In 1755, at Midhurst Mill, an earthquake 'rolled the waters forward and drove the stream backwards'. In 1833, 1834 and 1835 there was another succession of tremors at intervals over three months during which 'A stack of chimnies was shook down'. In 1864 there was a 'violent concussion' at Hurstpierpoint with a sound like wagons rumbling over cobbles and a 'wavy motion' of the ground. Most recently shocks were felt in 1984, when windows shook and china rattled.

These newspaper extracts vividly convey the impact of the earthquakes:

23rd September 1833
On Wednesday morning, about 10 o'clock, the inhabitants of Chichester and its neighbourhood, to an extent of several miles, experienced the shock of an earthquake. Although the agitation of the earth, and the rumbling sound which accompanied it, continued but for a moment, it was sensibly felt by almost every individual, and created a great degree of alarm; and we regret that a poor man, named Marshall who was digging at the time in a chalk pit near Cocking, was killed by the falling in of a quantity of chalk, supposed to have been loosened by the shock. An inquest has been held and a verdict of 'Accidental Death' passed.

16th November 1833
A smart shock of an earthquake was felt in Chichester and its vicinity on Tuesday morning between three and four o'clock. It was sufficiently severe to awaken almost everybody and even to cause the bell on the cross to give a single toll. This is the second event of this kind witnessed within two months in the same locality and some of the more timid are apprehensive of more serious results of which these slight shocks are really precursors. But all the earth is feverish and doth shake more than we have reason to expect in these latitudes.

Earthquakes are caused by instability in the earth's crust, and the presence of faults beneath Chichester will always make the area vulnerable to shocks and tremors. Overall 18 earthquakes have been recorded in the last 234 years.

Severe Winters

The most tangible, and most talked about, Acts of God are those inflicted by the weather. The winters of 1947 and 1963 stand out in people's memories as being particularly severe. There is no doubt that 1963 was the harder because temperatures were lower for longer periods, the wind-chill factor created by bitter easterly winds 'from Siberia' accentuated low temperatures, conditions were more extreme and the consequences were more far reaching. Lord Winterton wrote in 1947 that the worst he could remember was as a boy in 1895 when jugs of water in his bedroom froze solid.

The most visible consequence of the cold was the sudden appearance of winter sports associated with high altitude continental resorts as the football

league programme shut down for five or six weeks: skiing on the Downs, skating on ponds and lakes at Ashurst, Partridge Green and elsewhere, ice hockey on the lake in Petworth Park and the village pond in Storrington, curling on the Chichester Canal at Donnington and snowmen everywhere. Less conspicuous was the 'flying squad' of water tankers which circulated to answer the thousands of calls for water as pipes froze. When they thawed the lead pipes burst putting a huge strain on plumbing and building services. Coal stocks were low and supplies disrupted by the road conditions. Power cuts were regular occurrences and were compounded by a shortage of 'shillings' for the gas and electricity meters. Inevitably deaths from hypothermia and respiratory complaints increased. Food ran short and milk deliveries were impeded. One enterprising farmer drove his tractor and trailer around Southwater with churns of milk and on one occasion sold 800 gallons in less than three hours. Post and newspaper deliveries were made by sledge. Bus companies ran despite surfaces 'more suited to the Cresta Run' than roads. In the first two weeks over 9,000 tons of grit was spread and 1,100 tons of salt. Supplies had to be replenished by queueing at the salt mines in Cheshire.

2   *Skating on a frozen pond in Storrington in January 1963.*

3 *Skating on thin ice with a spaniel in Pagham Harbour in January 1963.*

4 *The frozen sea at Bosham on 3 February 1963.*

Most spectacular were the 20-ft snow drifts all over the county. Cars were trapped and abandoned. The weight of snow brought down guttering and broke the glass at nurseries. There were 20-ft ice floes on the River Arun at Arundel. It was possible to walk across the river near Ford railway bridge and it even froze at its mouth at Littlehampton despite the tidal range. Indeed, each tide simply added another layer of ice on top of what already existed. About fifteen schools closed for lengthy periods, and others for a shorter time because they could not be heated or pupils were unable to get to them. Theatres and cinemas closed because of dwindling audiences.

The County Council and other local authorities were stretched to the limit despite allocating 700 men and 300 pieces of snow-clearing equipment to keeping traffic moving. The A27 had to be closed because of frost-heave which lifted the surface as the frost expanded. The conditions were so bad that in clearing the roads stretches of 'cats eyes' were dislodged and swept up and had to be replaced at a cost of 13s. each. The overall cost exceeded £100,000, which in 1963 was a huge sum.

The Great Storm 1987

The cost of dealing with events which can be anticipated and for which preparations can be made in advance is dwarfed by the costs associated with unexpected occurrences which arrive with little or no warning, or even, as

5 *A car crushed by fallen trees along the A286 Chichester-Midhurst road after the Great Storm of 16 October 1987.*

6 A 'petrified' forest in Slindon Woods with the crowns sliced off by the ferocity of the winds during the Great Storm.

in 1987, assurances by weather forecasters that an exceptional storm would miss us.

Four hours of winds in excess of 100 m.p.h. in the early hours of Friday 16 October 1987 left a trail of chaos and destruction throughout West Sussex which took months to clear. The Fire Brigade received its first call at 2.03 a.m. and in the next 24 hours logged 1,129 calls, the amount it normally receives in two months. The structural damage to property was immense as houses shook, walls blew down, roofs were carried hundreds of metres, tiles flew everywhere, windows smashed, and anything not secured was lifted and deposited elsewhere. Temporary tarpaulin canopies were a frequent sight and services at Racton church continued under such cover.

The landscape changed overnight. Over three million trees were affected and it is planned to replant one million. The force of the wind uprooted huge trees and stripped forests bare of the crowns and branches. Patches looked like Armageddon or a petrified forest after a volcanic eruption. Some 40,000 trees fell across roads, yet the main roads had been cleared by Saturday

lunchtime. By mid-December there were still 1,000 tree trunks, 2,000 stumps and 2,500 loads of branches still awaiting removal and disposal to one of nine burning sites throughout West Sussex operating 24 hours a day. The County Council was still employing 95 per cent of its staff on clearing a month later. The market for timber collapsed as sawmills offered rock bottom prices. Overnight the Great Storm provided eight years' supply of walnut, two years' supply of sweet chestnut and 100 years' supply of beech.

The electricity and telephone networks were severely disrupted. Engineers had to be brought in from other parts of the country to reinstate services

7 *Uprooted trees lying across The Avenue, Summersdale, Chichester on the morning after the Great Storm.*

8 *Prince Charles in front of an uprooted tree, October 1987.*

as quickly as possible, but while most were reconnected within a week more isolated places were weeks without electricity. Twenty schools were still closed a week after the storm and another 20 were only working because mobile classrooms had been delivered to replace unusable buildings. Something like 20 per cent of the street lights were put out of action and over 23,000 timers had to be re-set. Their damage to glasshouses was catastrophic and one nursery in Barnham estimated that the clearance equated to picking up glass from 50 football pitches. Their aluminium frames were twisted and contorted into grotesque sculptures and had to be replaced.

The mopping up operation was masterminded from the emergency bunker beneath County Hall, Chichester which was also used when the city was flooded. The cost to the county has been estimated at £8.25 million and insurance claims topped £20 million. Disasters attributed to the weather are considered to be 'natural hazards' against which we can protect ourselves. The Great Storm 1987 and 'flash floods' warn against complacency and reinforce the message to be prepared for anything.

The Worst in Living Memory

Every storm seems to get labelled as 'the worst in living memory' or a 'once in a lifetime' occurrence. The 1987 hurricane warranted these descriptions and the Easter 1913 gale almost qualified for them too.

On 22 March a ferocious equinoctial gale, which coincided with the highest tide of the year, hit the West Sussex coast. The audience attending the evening's entertainment on Worthing Pier was evacuated just in time before massive waves caused the pier to crash into the sea. All that remained was the pierhead and a length of decking projecting defiantly into the sea. The shingle-carpeted coastal road resembled a causeway stretching between the sea and 500 acres of flooded land. The *Evening Argus* observed, 'The little township reminded one of a man who had suddenly become aged, toothless, crutched [*sic*] and tottering under a knockdown blow.' Worthing was plunged into darkness.

Further along the coast 15 railway carriage homes on Lancing beach were carried out to sea and a further 15 were irretrievably damaged. No lives were lost but one family rode the waves until the sea relented in the early morning. They were becalmed and it seemed hardly credible that a few hours previously the sea was 'battering Worthing to pieces'.

9 *Worthing Pier destroyed by a storm, 23 March 1913.*

10 *Telephone wires brought down by a storm in Haywards Heath, 1908.*

An enterprising businessman offered postcards of the devastation to the sightseers who flocked to the scene. Unfortunately sales were few and he explained, 'Everybody asks me "What is this and what is that" and I talk to them until I am as dry as (a very hot place) and then they says "Thank you kindly" and goes away.'

An almost equally severe gale and snowstorm in January 1908 brought down 30 iron standards and the overhead telephone wires in Haywards Heath. Miraculously there was no loss of life. The Council waged a campaign to put the wires underground but failed to convince the Post Office or the Postmaster General and they were replaced with wooden poles.

11 *Normal service was maintained at Chichester crematorium during the severe flooding in January 1994 despite its being under water.*

Flooding, a Natural Disaster?

Some places are prone to flooding, particularly those on the flood plains of rivers. In West Sussex the flat land to the south of Pulborough is regularly inundated by the River Arun as it overflows its retaining banks. Here, and at Amberley Wild Brooks lower down its course, the regular flooding constitutes an integral part of the ecosystem. Elsewhere flooding is less frequent and often unexpected.

In January 1994 'Operation Badminton' was triggered when Chichester was hit by a 1-in-200-year catastrophe. The evacuation of a large part of the south-east of the city was put in hand but averted through the efforts of the National Rivers Authority, West Sussex County Council, the Fire Brigade, Army and other emergency services who fought manfully to contain and divert the rampaging flood waters away from the city.

River Lavant is a 'winterbourne' or seasonal stream which usually flows from December to May/June but whose bed is dry for the rest of the year. Between 1990-3 it hardly flowed at all during a succession of dry years, but in 1993 a very wet autumn broke the sequence. Over 600mm of rain fell between 1 September 1993 and 1 January 1994, the yearly average in four months, raising the level of water in the ground. Springs normally dormant began to flow. Between Christmas Day and 10 January 1994 a further 200mm of rain fell, including 51 mm in four hours on 30 December. The December 1993 rainfall was 175 per cent above average.

12   *Flooding in Lavant and pipes snaking through Chichester and Singleton, January 1994.*

13 *Constable's painting of Middleton church in 1795 shows it perched on the edge of the sea.*

The aquifer formed by the chalk of the South Downs filled and became artesian as it burst out in springs never previously seen, including through the floors of houses, onto already saturated ground and into an overflowing River Lavant. The consequence of this combination of factors was widespread and deep flooding. The mousey little stream had roared.

The National Rivers Authority has measurements from a well at Chilgrove in the Lavant catchment going back 167 years, the longest record of this type in the world. Only a handful of times over that period have there been artesian flows and never on this scale, despite extraction of water from the chalk aquifer in the Downs never having been so high. In the 41 days between 1 December 1993 and 10 January 1994 the level in the well rose 27 metres. This was exceptional. At its peak on 12 January the River Lavant flowed at 8.0 cubic metres per second compared with the normal January flow of 0.46 cubic metres per second. Around 150 million gallons of water was flowing through or around Chichester every day. The first sign of a fall occurred on 20 January but the 'Lavant Flude' continued flowing at above average speeds and volumes well into March.

Damage was widespread, especially along the Lavant valley where the villages of East Dean, Charlton and Singleton were swamped. The culvert under the city centre was unable to cope and property and shops were flooded. The city centre was criss-crossed with pipes for months as pumping attempted to alleviate the danger. Fire Brigade resources were supplemented by 16 'Green Goddesses' to help pump water into Chichester Harbour, three kilometres away. They stayed in position into February. Over 220,000 sandbags and temporary dams offered some protection.

There was traffic chaos. The main A27 trunk road was closed and the A259 to Bognor Regis had to be raised on a bailey bridge over flood water which had found an outlet along an old river course to the sea at Pagham Harbour. This and other measures saved the city from more severe damage. The total cost exceeded £6 million. To prevent a repetition, a scheme of works initiated by the Environment Agency, intercepting the River Lavant before it reaches Chichester and diverting it to a new pumping station at the tidal Pagham Harbour, has been completed.

Coastal Erosion: Surrender or Fight them on the Beaches

Some disasters change the face of the countryside in a few devastating hours or over a relatively short period of time, while other processes operate insidiously day in day out. The alterations made by the daily tidal rhythm to the coastal zone are imperceptible to the naked eye but over time have redrawn the map.

The Sussex coastline has always receded. Actual and anecdotal evidence points to a rate of retreat of between 2.0 and 4.5 metres a year. In Bracklesham a quarter of a mile of the coast was lost in 150 years which, if it continued at the same rate, would have retreated 2½ miles in 1,500 years. At nearby Selsey the original cathedral and the bishop's deer park, part of which was still in existence in Tudor times, have disappeared beneath the sea. In 1846 a 95-year-old Kingston-by-Ferring man reminisced that in his youth an 80-year-old man had told him about Ruston Park, where elm trees were cut and sold at a farthing a foot but which was now under the sea.

Villages and churches lie beneath the sea. Camden, the 16th-century traveller, referred to New Shoreham, 'the greater part also being drowned'. Between Pagham and Worthing four villages, Middleton, Cudlow, Charlton and Ilsham, are known to have been drowned. Constable's painting of Middleton church (1795) shows it perched precariously on the edge of the coast just before it succumbed to encroachment by the sea in 1837. As early as the 1630s Middleton was 'much decayed, wasted and consumed with the sea whereof divers houses and landes are eaten away'.

The coastline is a constant battle zone. Global warming, rising sea levels, higher tides, and more frequent storm surges allied to a perceptible downward tilt of south-east England is bound to magnify the problems. The West Sussex coastline has been fixed by engineers since the 18th century but this has not prevented recurring incursions at vulnerable points such as Selsey Bill. The authorities responsible, such as the County Council and Environment Agency,

14 *Houses tottering on the brink of a low cliff overhanging the sea at East Wittering, 1966.*

15 *Sea defences near Selsey comprising groynes, imported rock reinforcements and hurdles to prevent direct attack and lateral drift.*

have conducted research and arrived at a strategy which offers four options:

1. Do nothing (allow nature to keep the coast in equilibrium by depositing as well as eroding)

2. Hold the line (a programme of defences to keep the sea at bay including groynes, beach replenishment, offshore rock islands, revetments and other structures)

3. Retreat the line (accept the inevitable and give up the most vulnerable land by means of a managed retreat converting it back to marshland and salt flats)

4. Advance the line (an aggressive approach requiring barriers and dykes to produce a coastal landscape reminiscent of the Netherlands)

Whichever option is adopted has huge resource implications. It is likely that a combination of all these will be necessary. The idea of ordered retreat has already been proposed for the tip of the Manhood peninsula, causing Selsey residents to forecast that 'Eventually we will finish as an island', which is a return to the situation when the Armada map was drawn (p.97). What is certain is that the powers-that-be cannot sit on the shore, Canute-like, and hope the problem will ebb away.

The Subsiding Spire

Occasionally individual buildings experience unexpected and sometimes inexplicable events. In this case a 'House of God' was the victim of an 'Act of God'. On 26 February 1861 Dean Hook addressed a public meeting and described the final hours of the Chichester Cathedral tower and spire before the city's 'chief ornament' collapsed:

> On Wednesday evening a gale set in making the tower and spire to rock and grind stones together, and wherever there was a crack, pouring forth constant streams of dust. Still the men worked vigorously and hopefully (to shore it up) not leaving the building until half past three in the morning. When they returned at half past six they found the woodwork severely strained ('buckled lke a wheel, bent like a bow and snapped like a dry stick'). At about twelve o' clock the case seemed hopeless. You know the rest. It is indeed Providence that no life was lost.

Premature recriminations and attributions of blame caused Dean Hook to caution against 'the wonderful stories of the last few days, which if not invented by malice, have been circulated by folly'.

The cathedral was undergoing restoration and enlargement, including the removal of the Bishop Arundel Screen and choir fittings, where services had 'hitherto been confined', to accommodate larger congregations. During this work it was discovered that the piers supporting the tower (built *c.*1200) and the spire (built about 200 years later) were filled with rubble and were totally inadequate to support the weight. As early as June 1860 'mischief began to spread fissures opening out considerably causing great anxiety'. The consulting engineer concluded that there was 'some risk but no immediate danger'. Depending on the definitions of danger, risk and immediacy, his advice was flawed. At half past one on 21 February 1861

16 Cathedral dignitaries and building experts inspecting the interior of Chichester Cathedral following the collapse of the spire on 21 February 1861.

the piers gradually gave way allowing the tower and spire to sink eerily, 'with little noise', into the nave of the cathedral in a mass 'as if it had fallen through a trap door'.

The reaction to the catastrophe was one of disbelief and grief: 'Our loss is deplorable'. In addition to personal tragedy there were wider implications. 'Art has lost the most symmetrical spire in England on which the eye of Her Majesty and His Royal Consort, when on the Isle of Wight, must have sometimes rested with delight. The loss is a national one for the mariner has lost a landmark which, for ages, has been his guide among the shoals and reefs of Selsey Bill.'

The meeting answered the question of 'What is to de done?' by resolving to erect a tower and spire exactly 'on the model of the first'. Mr Giles Gilbert Scott was appointed architect and a public appeal was launched with the Duke of Richmond as chairman of the Appeal Committee. An unsolicited £26,000 had already been promised to start the appeal.

The Builder of 1 June 1861 made a far sighted suggestion well in advance of its time by proclaiming that as august a body as the Building Institute should consider 'whether it be not desirable that some organisation analogous to the one which prevails amongst our neighbours (e.g. France) for the preservation of monuments connected with the history of the country should be introduced in England … As ancient buildings of a country are part of the "intellectual property" of the whole nation maintenance should not be left to local or casual efforts.' This was an early plea for the formation of a body such as English Heritage or the National Trust.

This poem was published in the *West Sussex Gazette*:

It has fallen. It has fallen, from its station on high
And our pride in it now is a pleasure gone by;
The light hearted child or the silver haired sire
Will gaze no more on our time honored Spire.

We loved to behold it when morning was nigh,

Or when evening's first star shone faint in the sky;
We loved to behold it when sunbeams were bright,
And to hold it close in the dusk of the night.

Oh how lovely looked City, and Minster, and Spire,
When the sun went down in a ball of fire;
When its light played over it, golden and rare,
Never again shall we see glancing there.

Like a beacon it spoke to us sweetly of home,
When distant and weary our footsteps might roam;
And ever projecting, majestic on high,
It pointed the way to our hopes in the sky.

We behold it alike from the wood covered steep
And away, far away, on the blue moaning deep;
It was dear to our hearts and beloved of our eyes,
Alas! no more will it mesmerise.

We'll miss it when Summer brings warmth thro' the land
And scatters her gifts with bountiful hand;
We'll miss it when ruthless Winter comes forth,
Like a conqueror armed with cold winds from the north.

Still, the sunshine may play round the grey, ancient town,
And the turrets of Goodwood look haughtily down;
The bells of the Minster still cheerfully chime,
For the City to rejoice in festival time.

But something familiar hath passed from the spot,
And the loss of its presence will ne'er be forgot;
Neither the light hearted child nor silver haired sire
Will gaze evermore on our time honored Spire.

Uppark, A Phoenix Rises from the Ashes

Disasters do not respect reputations or owners, whether monarchs or heritage bodies such as the National Trust. On a typical warm, windy late summer afternoon in 1989 the roofing contractor's leadworkers were taking their tea break on the lawn in front of Uppark House when they noticed a puff of smoke escaping beneath the roof pediment. At 3.36 p.m. the fire alarms went off inside the house. The remaining visitors were immediately evacuated and well-rehearsed fire procedures swung into action.

Eight minutes after the alarms went off smoke was billowing from the roof pediment on the east side of the building. A minute later the first flames were visible. The first fire engine arrived from Petersfield before 4 o'clock and within six minutes there were four fire engines in attendance and 16 on their way. At the height of the blaze there were 27 fire engines present manned by 157 firemen from West Sussex, Hampshire and Surrey. By 4.30 the attic was alight and by 5 o'clock the family apartments were ablaze as the fire spread down through the house. The crews managed to contain the fire in the upper floors reducing the damage to the state rooms on the ground floor.

Uppark's hill-top position posed a problem of water pressure and supply and water was already running out by 4.30. The problem was solved by employing five 5,000-gallon water carriers and a convoy of fire engines running a shuttle service. A lake at the bottom of South Harting Hill was harnessed and water was pumped up the hill.

Staff and volunteers began to evacuate pictures, furniture, textiles and fittings as soon as the smoke appeared, some running and some forming a human chain passing items away from danger. When the regional National Trust officers arrived around 5 p.m. the firemen responded to their request to make a final effort to extricate certain valuable objects. Wearing protective clothing they salvaged everything they could from the ground-floor state rooms despite the dangers posed by burning timber and showers of burning lead falling from the upper floors. As much as possible was taken under cover and conservators called in with bubble wrap, tissue paper, blotting paper and other protective materials, drawing on the experience of the Hampton Court fire in 1986.

17 *An aerial view inside Uppark showing how the upper floors had been gutted by fire, August 1989.*

By 6.30 it was too dangerous to enter the building. As night fell the silhouette of the house provided the backcloth to a picturesque scene of flickering flames, spitting and crackling wood, the drone of the pumps, tangled hoses snaking over the lawns and the intermittent thud of collapsed ceilings. At 3 a.m. the National Trust officials and chief fire officers ventured into the building to be confronted by an infernal mess. Daylight revealed the full extent of the catastrophe. The morning's headlines pronounced 'Uppark gutted' but this proved an exaggeration as much of the ground floor decorative wood and plaster, doors, marble fireplaces and chandeliers had miraculously survived.

It took five days before the fire was officially 'out' and until then a continuous watch and periodic 'damping down' was necessary. As soon as the 'all clear' was given the dirty and laborious process of sifting through the sludge for any fragments began. It was a painstaking task and the teams succeeded in retrieving 12,000 finds. The residue was put in 3,860 dust bins each referenced to the part of the house from which it was derived, because it was later sieved on a conveyor belt. Nothing that might help in restoration could afford to be discarded.

Three ballroom-size marquees were erected on the lawn to allow the sodden textiles to dry out naturally, with a little help from the conservators. Part of one tent was converted into a 'field hospital' where the injured bodies were stretched out on bead trays from the Red Drawing Room and

19 *Uppark House restored to its former glory, 2003.*

Little Parlour. The pathetic remains of four tassels and other victims were treated with tender loving care by the conservators, who worked for 14 hours a day seven days a week. The whole project engendered the 'blitz' spirit of working together, and a shared Monty Python menu of 'spam, spam, spam' and Mars bars consolidated the egalitarian team effort.

The walls remained intact, supported by the scaffolding which had borne the brunt of the year-long structural repairs and maintenance just drawing to a close. They needed further buttressing but were structurally sound. On 4 October 1989 the executive committee of the National Trust announced the decision to restore Uppark to the appearance of 'the day before the fire'. The photographic archive, surveys and inventories allied to the material recovered provided the basis of the restoration. The exhibition demonstrating the restoration and displaying skills and talents thought to have become extinct is an inspiration.

The decision was not universally welcomed and correspondence raged in the press. The arguments against were that whatever emerged would be a 'fake', a 'reproduction antique'. A local M.P., advocated demolishing Uppark and leaving it to nature. Another local M.P., of a different hue, responded by calling him 'the biggest Philistine since Goliath'. The proponents pointed to the heritage and promotion of the skills involved. The outcome was not a pastiche but a faithful resemblance of the original done so well that it gave the impression of having been untouched by a catastrophe of this magnitude. A prominent commentator claimed, 'Uppark is more than a restoration. It is an argument won.'

The cost, about £20 million, was met by the roofing contractor's insurers because contrary to instructions the leadworkers had left the roof prematurely and failed to detect that the timbers, on which the lead sheets were being welded, had ignited. They were considered to have been negligent.

Air Crash at Blackdown. No Survivors

Neither the collapsing cathedral spire nor the fire at Uppark involved loss of life, but casualties in transport accidents are often high. The occasional spectacular crash attracts more lurid headlines than the daily drip of deaths on the roads which is what ultimately gives statistics a frightening dimension.

Just after 10 p.m. on the evening of 4 November 1967 a Caravelle belonging to Iberian Airlines *en route* from Malaga to London Heathrow ploughed into the slopes of Blackdown Hill, narrowly missing Blackdown House and carving a corridor of devastation 400 metres wide. Beech trees were reduced to matchsticks and over 100 sheep killed as it bounced across the field where they were grazing. All seven crew and 30 passengers were killed instantly.

Fernhurst Village Hall was hurriedly converted into a makeshift mortuary where 15 bodies were laid out. In the carnage the other bodies were unrecognisable and severed limbs were strewn over the hillside. Eventually 25 persons were identified, mainly through dental records. The grim task of recovery was undertaken by over 100 members of the emergency services who were on the scene instantly, working by torchlight until emergency lighting was erected.

Market gardener Edgar Coles and his wife were watching 'The Univited Guest' on television when they heard the plane and the almighty thud as it hit the ground. They were unable to dial for help as the telephone wires had been cut. They rushed outside to see if they could offer assistance but were driven back by the ferocity of the blaze. They were horrified at the extent of the damage.

The black box was recovered and the cause of the crash attributed to human error but there was a suspicion that the altimeter had failed. A few minutes before crashing the pilot had received permission from air traffic control to reduce his height from 31,000 to 14,500 ft. and then to 6,000 ft. to begin his descent to Heathrow airport. The plane was on its projected flight path and due to land in 10 minutes. Just prior to the crash it was recorded at 9,000 ft. so how it hit Blackdown at 900 ft. remains a mystery. The coroner's verdict was 'death due to multiple injuries caused by Misadventure'.

The Runaway Train Crashes

The regulations of the London and Brighton Railway Company stipulated that no train was allowed to enter a tunnel until the previous train had passed through. To ensure they were observed through the 1¼ miles long Clayton Tunnel cut at a depth of 270 feet beneath the South Downs five

20 *A railway engine derailed at Cocking (1957) following the collapse of a bridge due to a deficient culvert.*

miles north of Brighton there were signalmen at either end who communicated with each other by a single needle telegraph.

On Sunday morning, 23 August 1861, an excursion train from Portsmouth, which had picked up passengers at Chichester and Worthing, left Brighton at 8.05 a.m. It was followed at 8.15 a.m. by an excursion train from Brighton to London and at 8.30 a.m. by the stopping train from Portsmouth to London which had picked up passengers along the coast. The first train was signalled through the tunnel by Harry Killick but had still not exited when the Brighton-London excursion train appeared. The trip signal jammed so the signalman waved a red flag to alert the engine driver that there was danger ahead. The driver, obeying the flag, shut off the steam and stopped about 200 yards inside the tunnel and began reversing towards the tunnel entrance to establish the problem. Harry Killick telegraphed the signalman at the exit, John Brown, to enquire if the train had come through. He received the answer 'Yes, train through' because the first train had come out, but the second, unknown to Harry Killick at the entrance, had halted. He assumed that it had not seen his flag to stop and continued through the tunnel, and gave the 'go ahead' signal to the third train which hit the second train, by now stationary in the tunnel, with 'thundering force', pressing the carriages of the Brighton-London excursion into a 'concertina'.

The engine reared up like a prancing horse and settled on top of the crushed rearmost coach of the excursion train. The final carriage bore the brunt of the collision and contained the bulk of the casualties. In a remarkably short time rescuers were on hand with emergency lighting to illuminate the

21 *The opening of the Shoreham branch line in 1844 with a train consisting of two first-class compartments with a coupe (single seat and observation windows) at either end, and dangerously overcrowded second- and third-class coaches. Even the tender accommodated cheering passengers. One man was killed when he fell off the luggage van.*

pitch-black tunnel. When they arrived they found a horrific amalgam of dead and dying. Some of the bodies had been maimed and mangled out of all recognition; two people had to have their legs amputated above the knee; a mother who had been feeding her baby had her breast ripped off; a man looking for his wife found her corpse sitting upright in her corner seat; others were trapped; more had been scalded by the boiling water from the tender; there were groans, yells, shrieks, and a great deal of praying; some were too shocked and frightened to move while others were running to and fro in panic. An eye witness said, 'I have never witnessed such a sight in my life and I trust to God never to do so again.'

The signalmen's error caused 22 deaths and injured 176. The bodies were laid out on Hassocks Gate station and then removed to the reading room at Brighton station where their remains were stretched out on planks and trestles and covered with sheets, any belongings placed at the feet of each body to assist identification. As each body was claimed the name of the victim was chalked at the feet. It was a scene of 'uncontrollable grief'. The nine seriously injured were taken to hospital. The newspaper report concluded, 'Let us draw a veil over this terrible accident; it is too shocking to dwell upon.' It is wise to heed this advice!

A similar calamity occurred in virtually the same place on 23 December 1899 when the Brighton-London Victoria Pullman, running late, ran into the back of the Newhaven-London boat train at Wivelsfield in 'one of the thickest fogs ever known', killing the guard and five passengers and injuring 19 people. The crash produced 'an awful wreckage and a piteous spectacle

22   *The old toll bridge, New Shoreham, opened in 1781/2.*

23   *The Norfolk Suspension Bridge, New Shoreham, 1832.*

of maimed and mutilated humanity'. The impact sounded 'as if a battery of artillery had opened fire on Burgess Hill'.

The guard's van of the Newhaven train and four carriages were shattered and telescoped while others rolled down the embankment. Two carriages caught fire. The 'permanent way' was torn up, the rails 'twisted like giant corkscrews', and wheels were found two fields away. Doctors arrived 'as if by magic' from all over mid-Sussex and treated the injured on the spot. The seriously injured were taken to Brighton or Guy's Hospital, London.

The inquest delivered a verdict of 'Accidental death' and in a judgement reminiscent of the different types of leaves on the track, they attributed the blame partly to the driver of the Pullman, who was 'negligent' but not 'grossly negligent', and partly to the density of the fog and the failure of the 'fogmen' to place detonators on the rails to warn advancing trains of the danger ahead. Other individuals were absolved of blame and it was recommended that 'understaffing' be rectified by appointing 'a second man or intelligent youth' to the main signal boxes, especially at Keymer, and recruiting more fog signallers 'within call of those responsible for employing them'.

Recommendations of inquests and enquiries are invariably adopted in an effort to placate anger and prevent repetitions, but 'Acts of God' have always undermined the best laid strategies of companies and organisations.

It's not 'Rocket' Science

To the memory of the Rt. Hon. William Huskisson, for 10 years (1812-23) one of the Representatives of this City [Chichester] in Parliament. This station he relinquished in 1823 when, yielding to a sense of publick duty he accepted the offer of being returned for Liverpool, for which he was selected on account of the zeal and intelligence displayed by him in advancing the Commercial Prosperity of the Empire.

24 *The first passenger railway from Liverpool to Manchester in 1830 was driven by George Stephenson's 'Rocket'. The Duke of Wellington's ceremonial carriage included William Huskisson, President of the Board of Trade and M.P. for Chichester 1812-23, who was the first railway passenger to be killed when the engine stopped to take on water during the fateful journey.*

His death was occasioned by an accident near the Town on XV of September MDCCCXXX [1830] and changed a scene of triumphal rejoicing into one of general mourning.

At the urgent solicitation of his constituents he was interred in the Cemetery there amid the unaffected sorrow of all classes of people …

This inscription is on the pedestal of a statue of Huskisson which stands in Chichester Cathedral opposite a memorial to his wife, Emily, who died at Eartham in 1856, where she lived and is buried.

A letter written by E.J. Littleton to the Marquess of Anglesey, Huskisson's close friend, a few days later gave this account of the accident:

We were waiting on the railway to take in water. It was in a large stone quarry through which a dam is raised for the railroad. This dam is very narrow, only allowing room for the double railroad – but no standing room on the sides. Huskisson was speaking to the D of W, who was standing inside at the head of the car – when the Duke observing the people re-entering the car said 'Well, we seem to be preparing to go – I think you had better get in.' I was standing close to Huskisson at the time, and on hearing the Duke say this, I turned around and saw an engine on the opposite railway coming at great speed – then about 200 yards distant. I got up on the side of one of the cars through the wicket, but not without difficulty, for it was very high, and there were no steps. I turned round and pulled in Esterhazy after me – I then saw Huskinsson in great trepidation seize the wicket, which was open, and try to get round it. He even lifted up his leg to try and enter, but it was too late. He had lost his head entirely – the engine had come up, and in trying to fling himself out of the way the engine knocked him down on his back in the centre of its road, but with his

25 *Eartham House, now Great Ballard School, Wm. Huskisson's home.*

left leg bent on the Rail so that the leg and thigh were crushed to a pulp, the bones quite comminuted. He was perfectly sensible from the moment of his accident to that of his death and bore his suffering with surprising fortitude and drawing the ear of those he wished to speak to down to his lips and giving directions about his Will etc.

Mrs Huskisson has reluctantly consented to part with his remains and that he should be buried with public honours at Liverpool. She is in the profoundest affliction. The corpse went from Eccles to Liverpool yesterday.

I have a letter from Palmerston full of grief on the occasion on public and private grounds. What a sad loss to the country.

William Huskisson, President of the Board of Trade, was killed by Stephenson's 'Rocket', the first victim of the steam engine. He was reluctant to desert Chichester because to him it symbolised cohesion and continuity, a prosperous past combining with a dignified and well proportioned present and no sense of sleepiness. He said, 'I cannot cast off Chichester as I would an old shoe.' He often wished he had remained in Chichester, because it was so quiet and complacent, rather than in the noise and bustle of the industrialising North West.

Yet he was proud of Chichester's nail making industry, which he saw as an industry of the stolid yeomen of Sussex whom he considered 'the salt of the earth'. Unlike John Wesley, who found 'their life supremely dull, and usually unhappy too. For, of all the people in the Kingdom they are the most discontented, seldom satisfied either with God or man.' Wesley failed to convert them, whereas Huskisson, preferring to consider them a 'subdued race', gained their full confidence and attributed the relatively low impact of agricultural unrest in the county in the 1830s to the wisdom of the Sussex farmers.

Huskisson bought William Hayley's house in Eartham (Eartham House, now Great Ballard School) where he and Emily found seclusion and extended generous hospitality to their friends. Indeed it has been said that it was in Eartham that 'he knew nearly all the happiness in his life'.

Two

HEALTH AND SAFETY

A Plague on the Sins of the Fathers

Historically, population has been kept under control by natural checks and balances, notably by outbreaks of contagious diseases which ravaged communities. Over time improvements in living conditions and medical science have combated the main killers and increased both life expectancy and the quality of life.

In 1603 England was visited by a recurrence of the Black Death. In London alone 37,000 died out of a total population of about 210,000. In 1665 London was hit again by the Great Plague, which killed 60,000. In the intervening period there were further outbreaks on a less dramatic scale. Leprosy was another scourge which killed many in West Sussex, including Zachary Gyllyn of Bury in 1613, while four burials at Treyford in 1853 were attributed to 'Black Vomit very much like Cholera'. Fairs and gatherings were cancelled. The coronation pageantry surrounding the accession of James I was curtailed and travel discouraged. Clergy apportioned blame to the sins of the fathers and preached that the pestilence was divine retribution.

Those with a less vested interest in implicating the Almighty correctly identified the cause as the unhygienic conditions and appalling filth that was found everywhere. In a society where a good wash was interpreted, even by monarchs and noblemen, as a 'lick and a promise', dead animals piled up in the streets attracting vermin, dung rotted, open sewers flowed between houses or formed stagnant pools, and in urban areas yellow acrid fumes, the product of burning sea coal, polluted the air. These conditions promoted the spread of diseases.

West Sussex was affected by the plague in 1563, when deaths were recorded in Chichester, 1603, when there were victims in the Sub-Deanery, Chichester, and 1665 in East Grinstead, and 1666 when Francis Pinion of Rogate and his entire family died from the disease. Rudgwick parish contributed to 'the relief of sufferers' throughout the country, including Charlbury (Oxon), Newport (Salop), Loughborough and Horsham, through 'special collections' called 'church briefs'. West Stoke sent a 'brief' to St Paul's, London during the Great Plague, and also relieved towns

26 *A plague doctor in his preventive uniform.*

devastated by fires such as New Alresford (Hants.) and Marlborough. Graffham contributed to Christian slaves in Algeria (1568), West Grinstead to translating the Bible in Lithuania (1661) and most parishes to named individuals in need. Parish records and church briefs are key sources for evidence of the plague and other diseases.

Single and repetitive plagues decimated communities and many villages became extinct as the remaining inhabitants left or were removed by landlords taking advantage of dwindling numbers to convert arable strip fields to more profitable sheep pastures.

Buried in 'Wollens'

An Act of 1666 and a more famous Act of 1678 decreed that,

> no corpse of any person (except those that shall die of the plague) shall be buried in any shirt, shift or shroud or anything whatsoever made or mixed with flax, hemp, hair, silk, gold, silver or in any stuff or anything other than what is made of sheep's wool only or be put into any coffin lined or faced with … any other material but sheep's wool only.

This transcript from the Rogate parish register 1691 illustrates how the Acts were implemented.

> Thomas Kingstone was buried
> the 12th day of January on a afadafit
> brought of his being –
> buried in woollands
> with in eight dayes 1691

The Act(s) required an 'affidavit' to be sworn, usually by a relative, within eight days of the funeral attesting that the law had been fulfilled. A £5 fine was levied if the person had not been buried in woollens. The Act(s) were not repealed until 1814 but compliance had long since lapsed and they had not been enforced for many years. The wealthier classes had long recognised it for what it was, a piece of legislation designed to protect the wool trade. They considered it a tax to be paid rather than as an injunction to be observed. The burial records of virtually every parish in West Sussex contain lists of parishioners 'buried in woollands'.

The Act was by no means unique. Almost a hundred years earlier, in 1571, another protectionist measure enjoined that 'all persons of common degree should wear woollen caps on Sundays' with a fine of 3s. 4d. to be levied for each transgression of the edict. The responsibility for policing the Act and collecting the fines was placed upon churchwardens. It was effective for 20 or 30 years but gradually fell into disrepute and was disregarded.

Smallpox, the most Serious Scourge

Smallpox was considered the most dangerous of the endemic fevers. The plague and typhoid did not occur as frequently as smallpox but incurred heavier losses during epidemics. Smallpox never really went away, recurring at frequent intervals with deaths in total exceeding those of the plague and typhoid. Smallpox became a killer disease in England in the late 16th century, accounting for approximately 20 per cent of total deaths in the 18th century.

It seemed to reach the parts that the plague and typhoid often missed.

27 *Tradition attributes a Pest(ilence) House on this site at Findon, where those with contagious diseases were quarantined from the early medieval period through to the 19th century.*

28 *St James leprosy hospital, Chichester was built in the 12th century, but destroyed by fire and re-built in the 18th century to the same plan on the same site using as much of the original material as could be salvaged.*

29 *James Gillray (1757-1815) caricatured Edward Jenner, who first demonstrated (1796) that inoculation with 'cow-pox' could protect against smallpox, being overwhelmed in his clinic for the poor. Parliament had just grudgingly granted Jenner £10,000 to maintain and develop his ideas.*

Deaths from smallpox were recorded much more frequently in villages and rural parishes than other fevers. Registering the cause of death was first made compulsory in 1837, although parish registers often detailed the cause of death prior to this date. London and rural Sussex often came together as a consequence of these infections:

> Thomas Woodcock, gentleman and patron of the church of Newtimber died 13th September 1665 and was at his dear wife's charge and advice of his faithful friend Mr Thos Ambler, then rector, reposed in a vault prepared for his corps to remain in until they could according to his desire and instruction by conveyed to London (where it should please God to heale the citye of ye Plague then most grievously raged there) to be interred in the Parish Church of All Hallows the wall but the sayd pestilence continuing so long even until the end of February following, here he resteth.
>
> John Merchant, the painefull tenant of the above named Mr Thomas Woodcock died of ye smallpox 1665.

Smallpox was a constant drain on parish rates. The overseers' accounts for Arundel in 1693 provide details of the relief given in a representative outbreak:

Widow Breamen having the small pox	2s. 0d.
Anne Avory being a tender, fortnight with Goody Breamen	3s. 0d.
Goody Breamen while sick	1s. 0d.
Widow Breamen while sick at times	2s. 6d.
Widow Hambleton and Widow Breamen for wood	2s. 0d.
Widow Hambleton sick of the small pox	4s. 0d.
Anne Avory tending Widow Hambleton three weeks	10s. 6d.

30 *St Mary's Hospital, Chichester was founded in the 12th century as an almshouse and night refuge and has stood on its present site since 1285. The internal plan is unique. It still houses 12 elderly almspeople.*

Apart from isolation, most parishes concentrated on cleanliness and getting premises 'fitt and sufficiently aired', and apparently providing some comfort. For instance, at West Hoathly in 1714 the overseers and churchwardens supplied a victim with 'candles, a saucepan, two pots, soap, starch, tobacco and pipes'.

Chichester was unhealthy, 'being too near the marshes and rather damp', and prone to flooding by the River Lavant. This was given as a contributory reason for the succession of smallpox outbreaks in the 18th and 19th centuries. In 1722, 994 people were infected, of whom 168 died. In 1740, 41 died from smallpox and the council set up a 'Pest House' to quarantine victims; in 1759 another 180 died, and in 1775 the All Saints parish register recorded,

Smallpox by contagion	43	
Smallpox by inoculation	1,611	of which 24 died
Remain unaffected	94	
	1,748	
Had Distemper before	2,465	
Died by inoculation	19	

Inoculation had been introduced in the early 18th century and became popular, despite the cost, with peripatetic 'inoculators' travelling the county. It helped reduce deaths and control outbreaks but the vaccine and techniques were suspect and numerous deaths were attributed to inoculation.

31 *Sackville College, East Grinstead, an almshouse built by the 2nd Earl of Dorset in 1619.*

Nevertheless, the practice appealed to the overseers and church-wardens to appease parishioners and suppress panic. The records of the Tillington overseers illustrates how they employed inoculators from time to time:

1789 Pd Mr King towards inoculating Hedgers and Kings children   £1 os. 9d.
1792 Pd Dame King for inoculating Rapson's family   £1 6s. 3d.
1792 Pd Mr Oliver for inoculating Hall's, Sageman's
        and Leggats family   £3 18s. 9d.
1801 Pd C. Ellis for G. Bryde for inoculating of his girl   5s. 3d.

Robert Sutton and his son Daniel invented a method involving a small puncture instead of a deep incision and they claimed to have treated 55,000 people in the south of the county between 1760-7, only six of whom died. In conjunction with the authorised practitioners were 'amateurs' such as Pearce, a local farmer in Bosham, who 'learnt the technique from his father'. Over a similar time span he inoculated about 1,000 people, charging 2s. 6d. to 5s. each, without incurring a single death. Such a paying proposition soon attracted other opportunists and a knife grinder, a fishmonger, a whitesmith and 'sly poachers of the other sex' rivalled the service he offered by undercutting his prices and exploiting gaps in the market.

Eventually vaccination replaced inoculation, and with improvements in living conditions, especially sanitation and water supply, the disease was

LOST, FOR A LONG TIME PAST,
In Clouds of Dust,
THE WATER CARTS
OF THE TOWN OF WORTHING.

WHOEVER will find them, and set them to work for the comfort and convenience of the Inhabitants, will be liberally Rewarded :---

NOT by the Local Board of Health;
But by the Tradesmen especially.

Worthing, 20th April, 1855.

32 *A handbill criticising the authorities for being dilatory in providing water carts to damp down the dust before roads were surfaced; and their response.*

brought under control. The last death from smallpox recorded in West Sussex was in 1928. The advances in medicine allied to improvements in public services shifted attention to domestic and personal hygiene. The emphasis stimulated the invention and manufacture of 'labour saving' devices designed to keep homes clean. The 'Whirlwind' cleaner carpet sweeper, manufactured in Billingshurst, lifted dust from carpets more efficiently than by hand and was typical of the new products. Inventors and entrepreneurs targeted the emerging domestic market.

NOTICE!!
THE WATER CARTS

Advertized as being lost on Saturday last, are in the hands of the Painter; should they be sufficiently dry, or no Rain set in, to risk their being spoilt by the dust, their appearance in the Streets may be expected in the course of a few weeks.

By order,

RICHARD LOCK.

Worthing, 23rd April, 1855.

From earliest times the Church had provided refuges or almshouses where the vulnerable, such as the elderly, could live in a community with a level of protection. St Mary's Hospital, Chichester is one of the oldest surviving medieval almshouses in Europe. Aristocrats, such as the 2nd Earl of Dorset who built Sackville College, East Grinstead in 1619, and other philanthropists bequeathed money for the establishment and running expenses of almshouses. There were usually conditions attached to the selection of residents and the provision only touched the tip of the iceberg, so a succession of Poor Law regulations was aimed at the majority unable to avail themselves of the shelter of the almshouses.

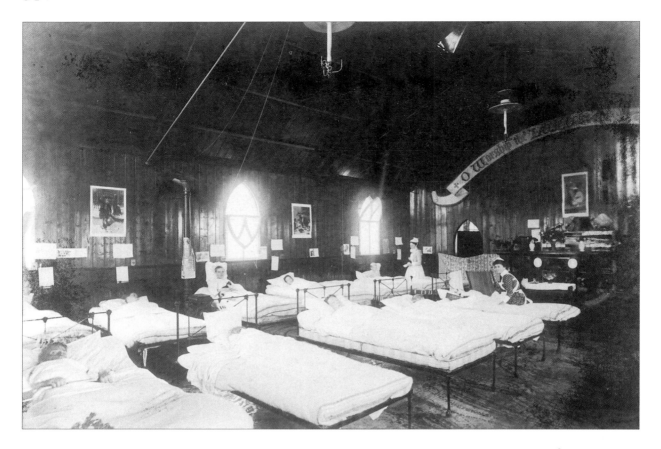

33 *The Methodist Church in Lyndhurst Road, Worthing was converted into temporary hospital accommodation during the typhoid epidemic in 1894.*

An Epidemic of Enteric (Typhoid) Fever in Worthing in 1893

Hygiene continued to be an issue well into the 20th century. The municipal sanitation and water undertakings which came into being towards the end of the 19th century had teething problems and standards were often compromised in the interests of 'dividends'.

An outbreak of typhoid hit Worthing in May 1893, peaked in July and was over by the end of November. In those seven months it created havoc as 1,416 inhabitants contracted the fever, nearly one in ten of the population, and 188 people died. The most vulnerable group were those between five and 20 years old. The outbreak coincided with an exceptionally long dry spell from 2 March to 4 July. The rest of July was wet but August was a hot, dry month. These were optimum conditions for harbouring and spreading the disease.

There had been early warning signs of a major outbreak, with minor outbreaks in 1865 due to defective sanitary arrangements, in 1880 due to contamination of milk in a specific dairy, and again in 1892. The blame for the 1893 outbreak was attributed to contamination of the water supply. The wells were capped and a new source of water was tapped at the foot of the

34 *Inside the soup kitchen in Grafton Street, Worthing during the typhoid epidemic of 1894.*

Downs near Broadwater; a new main was laid in ten weeks to connect with the existing system.

While this work was proceeding 180 galvanised water tanks, each holding 100-150 gallons and raised 18 inches off the ground on bricks, were placed strategically around Worthing, while ten large water carts circulated continuously around the town on a 'stop me and fill up' basis. Great care was taken to boil the water and sterilise the tanks and vans.

Worthing Infirmary set aside nine beds to meet the emergency and erected two tents in the grounds, each containing eight beds. This proved to be hopelessly inadequate so six large buildings were commandeered immediately and the Methodist Chapel in Lyndhurst Road was converted in 12 hours to house 26 patients. Altogether 228 beds were provided and 431 patients were admitted for treatment.

35 *A handbill advertising the availability of soup.*

Mortality was higher in hospital than among patients treated at home by a peripatetic army of nurses specially recruited to meet the demand and supplied with hired pony carriages and bicycles to enable them to carry out their tasks. At the height of the epidemic Worthing was divided into 14 districts and the nurses were allotted to particular sectors. In neighbouring parishes

SOUP for the POOR.

The Poor of the Parish of Broadwater will be supplied with SOUP at ONE PENNY per Quart, every TUESDAY, THURSDAY, and SATURDAY, by applying at the Soup Rooms, Market Street, between the hours of 12 and 1. Commencing on THURSDAY next.

Soup Committee Room,
Market Street, Worthing.
March 2nd, 1858.

Wilkins & Patching, Printers.

36 *The pediment of the Soup Kitchen in Grafton Street, Worthing topped by the figure of charity, with an inscription testifying that the Provident and Relief Society had been active since 1802 alleviating poverty and hunger.*

37 *A letter to the* Worthing Intelligencer *from a dairyman absolving himself from blame for the typhoid outbreak.*

BREAD AND PURE WATER.

To the Editor of the Worthing Intelligencer.

DEAR SIR,—A report is current that I manufacture my bread from the Worthing water. I beg to contradict that statement most emphatically, as the water I use is from the same well that has been in use now 30 years, and where the well water is drank we have not a single case of typhoid in the whole village—a sufficient proof of its purity.

I remain,
Your obedient servant,
J. B. KNOWLES.
South House, Broadwater,
July 20th, 1893.

such as West Tarring and Broadwater the Reading Rooms and Schools were converted into temporary hospital accommodation.

The effect on Worthing, which was marketing itself as a 'Health Resort', was catastrophic. Visitors shunned the town and business was negligible. Worthing became a 'Ghost Town'. The Mayor set up an 'Emergency Fund' to offset the losses, especially amongst the 'Lodging House Keepers' who had lost their source of income. Their rents were waived for three, six or nine months according to circumstances and they were supplied with free food and fuel. In an attempt to alleviate wider hardship and suffering the Provident and Relief Society placed its 'Soup Kitchen' at the disposal of the Mayor's Committee, which ran it for 24 weeks at a cost of £1,128 7s. 5d. The committee also met up to 30 per cent of the cost of funeral expenses and took over two buildings to provide convalescent care for 181 people. This was in addition to the Poor Law Convalescent Home for the paupers. The total sum disbursed by the Mayor's Fund amounted to £8,803 4s. 11d.

A revealing insight into the Worthing typhoid outbreak was given in 1977 by Mrs Edith Anderson, aged 97 years, who acknowledged that she was 'a great age but had a wonderful memory' and recalled details omitted from newspaper reports:

The filth that came from the tap was terrible, one dare not use it. (I think this is very hush hush but the sewer from The Infirmary sank into our water works.) We would walk out with jugs and kettles to collect water from the water carts. Oh for fresh water.

The Mayor and Councillors had a very rough time; their houses had to be boarded up as the men were very angry. When parents had the fever the children went to an office in South Street where they were given vouchers for the butcher, baker, grocer and dairy. November was a terrible month. The bonfire boys had a torchlight procession meeting at the Town Hall, the chief rider on a white horse; his attendants on horses rode through the town hoisting effigies of the Mayor and Councillors. When they got back to the Town Hall the effigies were set alight, very few went out, people were very frightened, then they had a big bonfire on the beach. I am sorry my writing is so awful but my eyes are tired.

There was no school, no bath nights so we ran to the sea to wash (it was a very hot summer) it was so clear we would roll in it. The doctors and nurses worked very hard, the doctors in a horse and trap and the nurses on bikes. Everyone went to church to pray for a return of normal times, everywhere was so silent. People put cards on their doors to warn that they had the fever and to keep out. People were dying very quickly, the undertakers used to take the bodies from the houses at night. There were funerals all day and every day, Sundays from dawn to dusk, cremation was not thought of. I think I have told you all I know!

Gas, Water and Electricity

Public 'utilities' represent one of the most significant advances in health and quality of life. They were launched by private companies in urban areas in the second half of the 19th century in response to government legislation and public pressure.

In 1866 the Burgess Hill and St John's Common Gas Company was formed at a public meeting with a capital of £5,000 in £5 shares. Initially the scope of the venture was limited to an area 1¼ miles from St John's parish church but the numbers of domestic consumers doubled in no time and the public lamps in the town centre were lit by gas. An arrangement well in advance of its time was a profit sharing and 'share option' scheme enjoyed by the employees.

In 1870 the Burgess Hill and St John's Common Water Company Limited was formed to ensure a regular supply of 'pure water' from taps instead of unreliable wells, streams and rain-storage receptacles which had previously sufficed. By 1874 there were only 214 customers but the growth of the town necessitated a succession of Burgess Hill Water Acts and Orders between 1871 and 1925 and the enlargement of the works and pumping

38 *The 'founding fathers' of the St John's Common Water Company, Burgess Hill, 1870 were all prominent local businessmen.*

39 *The Arundel Haven Harbour Commissioners launching the boat for a tour of inspection in 1887 with William Sewell, Harbour Master, at the flag. The rivalry between ports continued for over a century from the appointment of the Commissioners in 1732. Ship owners, captains and merchants repeatedly petitioned to transfer the port functions to Littlehampton but as more Commissioners came from Arundel these efforts were thwarted until 1864, when the Customs House was transferred to Littlehampton. Arundel did not cease to be a port until 1927. The 'bowler' hats introduced by Thomas Bowler in the middle of the 19th century were almost a 'badge of office'.*

stations and extension of the mains in order to keep pace with population increase.

In the 1850s complaints and representations were made to the Cuckfield Board of Guardians regarding the unsatisfactory sanitary conditions in Burgess Hill, particularly the dangers of stagnant water, cesspools, bad drains, and pollution of natural watercourses and ponds. Under the Public Health Act 1873, Poor Law Unions were compelled to appoint a Medical Officer of Health and a Sanitary Inspector. In 1879 a Local Board was formed in response to the Local Government Act in order to remove the hazards to health. It took until 1886 before the Medical Officer gave the town 'a clean bill of health', by which time Burgess Hill was promoting itself as a 'health resort' with hydros and spas.

In 1906 the Burgess Hill and District Electric Supply Company switched on the local lights which replaced candles and oil lamps. The first 50 horse-power dynamo was capable of lighting 1,000 lamps. Five years previously the

Burgess Hill Urban Council obtained the Burgess Hill Electric Lighting Order 1901 but failed to implement its provisions. The privately financed company filled the vacuum and flourished as the town expanded and additions were required to the generating plant to fulfil the demands. It was not until the 1930s that they tapped into the Central Electricity Board's Grid System.

The significant aspect of the incipient utilities is that they were private initiatives inspired and inaugurated by 'local worthies' investing in their home town. The names of the early 'directors' frequently turned up on the boards of all the local public utilities. Gradually the task of serving burgeoning communities became too onerous and private/public partnerships were a prelude to a public takeover of the provisions. This pattern was repeated in virtually every urban area, marking the transition from piecemeal provision to amenities now taken for granted. It was a seminal period in urban development.

40 *Richard 'Dickie' Carver lighting a gas lamp in Lombard Street, Petworth in the 1880s.*

Temperance

Drunkenness was the scourge of the 19th century; the overwhelming majority of cases appearing before magistrates were drink related. Alcohol was a major contributory factor to most of the evils of the Victorian period such as poverty, ill-health and crime, but it was an escape for working-class men and the pub was the focus of their lives.

In 1833 the Royal Commission appointed to enquire into the 'Swing Riots' observed 'the beer shops are considered most mischievous. They allow secret meetings in obscure situations in places kept by the lowest class of persons where stolen goods are exchanged and are frequently brothels.' The Beer Act 1834 attempted to ensure only 'respectable' persons were granted licences. An amendment in 1838 introduced stricter conditions and the replacement of beer shops by 'inns', which had a wider remit, but

41 *The elaborate 19th-century gas lamp in Petworth was designed by Sir Charles Barry, architect of the Houses of Parliament.*

magistrates simply granted licences to former beer shop keepers.

In this climate an influential Temperance Movement grew up to combat the evils of drink. The first attempt to establish a Temperance Society in Worthing occurred in 1840, when a number of people 'signed the pledge' to curb their drinking habits. Members were abused and attacked and met opposition from the authorities: the Local Board refused to hire the Town Hall for meetings. Despite this hostility the movement caught on and began to advocate total abstinence. By 1863 it had become sufficiently established for the Sussex and Surrey United True Temperance Society annual meeting to be held in the town. By the 1870s it had become probably the most influential pressure group in the country.

In the 1880s the Worthing Branch of the Working Women's Temperance League attracted a great deal of attention as it offered a route for women onto the political stage. Six months after its launch it drew an audience of over 400 to listen to rousing speeches and personal testimonies by the local organisers. The audience, mainly female brick workers, joined lustily in singing 'Rescue the Perishing' and other songs with a message. They defused all attempts at interference by men who invaded their meetings and indeed boasted that they had persuaded many men who had come to mock them to sign the pledge.

In Burgess Hill there were well attended lectures on 'Teetotalism', 'Drunkenness a cure' and other temperance subjects. Annual fêtes were entertained by a dedicated brass band. The movement was not confined to towns as the description of the evils of drink alongside the *Black Bear* in Kirdford demonstrates opposite.

Drunkenness had become so pervasive that even the Established Church was forced to act. Observance of the Sabbath was being neglected in favour of 'frivolities', especially drinking. Groups of clergy resolved to tackle the problem through their parishioners and by ensuring the churchwardens did the job for which they were appointed, which included visiting public houses and beer shops during divine service to apprehend those who were not attending.

In 1841 the farmers and tradesmen of Pulborough joined forces to reinforce the efforts of the Church:

> We the undersigned Tradesmen of Pulboro and its neighbourhood are disposed to feel anxious to close our shops on the Sabbath Day provided that the farmers will render us their assistance by settling with their labourers so as to enable them to shop during the week.

We the undersigned Rector, Churchwardens and Farmers of Pulboro and its neighbourhood do consider that Sabbath Trading ought to be abolished and will assist all in our power to enable the Trade to close their Shops on that Day by paying our Labourers at or before 12 o clock on Saturday mornings to enable their Wives to go the Shops previous to the Sabbath Day!

Shops will be closed on Sunday 14th February 1841 and will continue to be closed on every succeeding Sabbath Day.

The experience in Pulborough and Warnham was repeated throughout West Sussex. Traditionally, agricultural labourers were paid when they finished work on Saturday afternoon and devoted the evening to drinking it away. If there were any money left their wives could go shopping on Sunday. The triple effect on the household, the shops and church attendance led to the appeal to pay wages on Fridays so that wives could go shopping on Saturdays and there would be no excuse to miss church on Sunday. The Lord's Day Observance Society was a national movement arising from the abhorrence of the drinking culture and the measures taken at the parish and village level to break the vicious circle which perpetuated poverty and deprivation.

42 *The plaque alongside the former public house, the* Black Bear *at Kirdford, denouncing drunkenness.*

Vermin

The role of rats in spreading the plague is well known but what is less well known is an Act of 1532/3 which required every parish and township to provide a net to catch and destroy rooks, crows and choughs. The lord of the manor or landowner had to pay two pence for every 12 old crows, choughs or rooks. In 1566 the Act was renewed and extended to the destruction of 'Noyfull Fowles and Vermyn'. The churchwardens and six other parishioners were charged with assessing all landowners and holders of tithes to build up a fund to pay a penny for every three heads of old crows, choughs and rooks, a penny for every six young owls and a penny for every six unbroken eggs. The heads of the birds and animals and the eggs had to be shown to the wardens before receiving payment and then destroyed. The

43 *The Horsham Fire Brigade's Gala in 1881, where the brigade advertised allegiance to various insurance companies.*

Act was further extended in 1572/3 and 1597/8 to include sparrows at a rate of 1s. 6d. per dozen and hedgehogs.

The provisions of these Acts persisted well into the 19th century and the principles are still applicable today. The intention was to restrict damage to crops and sustain the supply of food. An entry in the parish register of Lyminster in the Arun valley for 5 May 1834 reads:

> The undersigned agree to kill 12 sparrows each week and produce them at the Monthly Parish Meeting and each defaulter is to pay 2d. for each dozen he may be deficient and any money to be spent by the meeting
>
> Jac Duke
> Thomas Duke
> John Babcock
> Wm. Osborne
> Geo Drewett
> Wm. Duke

We the undersigned Parishioners of Warnham, desirous that our Labourers should have the full enjoyment of the Sabbath day without its being encroached upon by worldly traffic, declare it to be our intention with God's blessing, to pay their weekly wages, from the date below inserted, on Friday Evening in each succeeding week instead of Saturday as heretofore.

March 1.. 1843 –

The terms are identical with those specified in the original Act over 300 years earlier, and the number of parishioners also coincides with the six which originally assisted the churchwarden to arrive at an assessment. By 1834 the parish had assumed both the responsibility initially placed on the churchwarden to implement the Act and the payment once made by the landowners. The six signatories were office holders in the parish, including overseers, confirming the status of the job and the potential reward. Parish meetings held at the *Six Bells* public house in subsequent years renewed the pledge to kill sparrows and there is only one case where a marksman fell short of his target. Retaining sparrow heads and eggs for up to a month as proof of the cull was hardly conducive to health, however.

44 *A commitment from parishioners in Warnham to pay wages on Friday instead of Saturday to co-operate with the clergy in keeping the Sabbath holy.*

Mental Health – Asylum Seekers

> Building site wanted for a lunatic asylum for the county of Sussex. From 50 to 100 acres on a dry soil and with a southern exposure, with a good supply of pure water; within two miles of a railway station on the main line, or else in a central position in regard to the divisions of the county … Parties having such land to offer are requested to communicate full particulars with price on or before 14th day of June 1854.

> *Sussex Advertiser,* 31st May 1854

In August 1854 Mr Grainger, a medical inspector with the Government Board of Health, alighted from the London-Brighton train at Haywards Heath station to be met by two members of the Committee of Visitors for the prospective Sussex Lunatic Asylum and two labourers with spades. He was to inspect possible sites, report and make a recommendation on the most suitable location.

OBSERVANCE OF THE LORD'S DAY.

AT A MEETING of the CLERGY of the RURAL DEANERY of HORSHAM, held at the VICARAGE, on Wednesday, 18th May, 1842, under the sanction of the Lord Bishop of the Diocese, and of the Venerable the Archdeacon of Chichester, it came under the consideration of the Clergy assembled whether something could not be done towards ensuring a stricter observance of the Lord's Day in their respective Parishes, and a more general attendance on the ordinances of religion,

IT WAS ACCORDINGLY RESOLVED,

1.—That, by God's help, *we will ourselves* exhibit to our respective flocks a uniform example of sanctifying *His* day by personal and domestic observance of the fourth commandment;

2.—That all Shopkeepers, and Dealers of whatever kind, be recommended strictly to abstain from all worldly traffic on the Lord's day;

3.—That the Gentry, Farmers, and others, from whom the Labouring Classes derive their means of subsistence, be requested to pay their labourers their wages, as far as in them lies, on Friday instead of Saturday night or Sunday morning;

4.—That the Gentry, Farmers, and respectable Householders, be earnestly invited to co-operate with the Churchwardens in preventing or dispersing all idle or noisy persons lounging about the streets and thoroughfares, especially in the approaches to Church, on the Lord's day; and in promoting by their own example, and by the best means their judgement suggests, a regular attendance on the Church Services, and the scriptural observance of the Sunday in their respective Parishes, among those over whom they have authority or influence;

5.—That the Churchwardens be reminded of their duty to visit, more frequently than is commonly done, the Public Houses and Beer Shops in their several Parishes, during the hours of Divine Service; and that the Constables and Headboroughs be called on to pay due attention to such houses at other times of the day; and especially that they be closed in the evening at the time prescribed by the late Act of Parliament.

6.—That the keepers themselves, of such houses, be requested to use their utmost exertions, that no just offence may be taken at their conduct in these respects; assured that the diligent observer of the Lord's day generally thrives in this world; and the neglecter of it, very seldom, throughout the whole of his life; and above all, that "Them that honour God, He will honour;"

7.—That all persons engaged in the public conveyance of Goods, and driving of Cattle, on the Lord's day—as also persons sending off their Waggons and Teams in the evening of that day, be strongly urged to abstain from such sinful conduct; and that they and all our parishioners be affectionately solicited to forbear in future from all unnecessary employment of their horses, needless journeys, and such and every profanation of the day of sacred rest.

BELOVED BRETHREN,

We, the appointed ministers of Christ to you, commend to your serious attention the above suggestions, hoping they will be received as they are given, in a spirit of kindness. And that God's Holy Spirit may incline and enable you to carry them into effect, to His honour, who is the Lord of the Sabbath, and our only Saviour, is the earnest prayer of

Your sincere friends and servants, for Christ's sake.

JOHN FISHER HODGSON, *Vicar of Horsham, Rural Dean.*
EDWARD ELMS, *Rector of Itchingfield.*
GEORGE BLAND, *Rector of Slinfold.*
GEORGE MATTHEWS, *Vicar of Rudgwick.*
JAMES WOOD, *Vicar of Warnham.*

WILLIAM ADAMSON, *Curate of Slinfold.*
HENRY ALLEN, *Chaplain of the Gaol, Horsham.*
ALEXANDER H. BRIDGES, *Minister of St. Mark's, Horsham.*
JARVIS KENRICK, *Curate of Horsham.*

WEST SUSSEX MENDICITY SOCIETY.

Resolutions suggested for a MEETING to be held at the COUNCIL CHAMBER, CHICHESTER, on THURSDAY, OCTOBER 22nd, 1874, at 3 o'clock.

I.—That a MENDICITY SOCIETY be established for the Western Division of the County of Sussex, with a Central Committee for the whole Division, and a Local Committee for each *Petty Sessional* Division.

II.—That the principle of the Society be the limitation of Relief to necessary food only, instead of Money or other alms, and that this be effected by means of Tickets, to be given to Vagrants on their applying for charity. Such Tickets to be exchangeable at some shop in towns or villages to be fixed on by the Local Committees. Such relief not to interfere with the relief now given in the Workhouses, in the way of lodging and food while there.

III.—That the Central Committee consist of the Chairman and Deputy-Chairman of Quarter Sessions, the Mayors of Boroughs, two Justices from each Petty Sessional Division, and two Guardians from each Board of Guardians, being Subscribers—three to form a quorum.

IV.—That the Local Committee consist of all Subscribers resident in the Petty Sessional Division; and meet four times a year, viz.: the last Bench-day in December, March, June, and September, at the place where the Petty Sessions are usually held, and at such other times as they may see necessary—three to form a quorum. At their first Meeting in each year they shall appoint a Chairman and Vice-Chairman, whose business it shall be to call any Meetings by advertisement in the County Paper, except those above mentioned.

V.—That the Local Committees be requested to meet on such early day as may be convenient for appointing the places where the Bread Tickets may be exchanged—such places to be at a distance of five miles or thereabouts—for the distribution of the Tickets, and such other business as may be requisite.

VI.—That the Public be earnestly requested to abstain from giving Money or Direct Relief to Tramps, and that Circulars and Bread Tickets be forwarded to the County and Borough Magistrates, to the Clergy of all Parishes, the Guardians of the Poor, Clerks to Justices, Clerks to Boards of Guardians, and Subscribers.

VII.—That Relief be only given by the Shopkeepers once for any number of Tickets presented by the same Tramp; such relief to consist of one pound of bread.

Subscriptions in aid of this Society, not exceeding s. nor less than 2s. 6d., will be received at the several Banks throughout the County, as also by the Honorary Treasurer, and the Honorary Secretary.

46 *The formation of the West Sussex Mendicity Society, in 1874, with its rules extending care to the most vulnerable in society, in this case tramps.*

45 *A resolution from the clergy in the Rural Deanery of Horsham in 1842 on Observance of the Lord's Day.*

Haywards Heath was, at this date, a virtually deserted open tract of country with a population of barely 200. Grainger arrived with a standardised format laid down by the Lunacy Commission which had been established to implement the 1845 Act requiring every county to open a lunatic asylum to house pauper lunatics currently disbursed throughout the county and beyond in various institutions, but especially in workhouses.

The specifications included a good water supply capable of providing each resident with 40 gallons a day (equivalent to a bath filled to the rim), seclusion and limited public access, and proximity to the main line railway station. The labourers dug test pits eight to ten feet deep to ascertain the soil quality and local health records were examined. The eventual purchase of the 120-acre Hurst House Farm in 1855 for £5,750 was a surprise as it was not the site recommended by Grainger; indeed he hadn't even visited it!

However it was cheaper, within a mile of Haywards Heath station on an eminence facing south, and the owner was a friend of one of the Committee of Visitors! Moreover, it satisfied the key criteria, especially being central to both East and West Sussex.

The architect chosen, Mr Kendall, was also the cheapest by over £10,000, the reasons for which became apparent from the defects that subsequently arose. He had to conform to the guidelines produced by the Lunacy Commission and planned a three-storey 408-patient (124 in single rooms and 284 in dormitory accommodation) asylum along conventional lines, with separate entrances for males and females flanking a main central entrance.

Sussex prevaricated for so long that it was the last county to build and open a lunatic asylum. Arguments ranged from costs and distance from relatives to questioning the value of medical treatment for 'idiots and imbeciles'. Eventually, increasing numbers of pauper lunatics, 455 in 1853,

NOTICE.

WHEREAS frequent complaints have been made to us of the assemblage of many idle and disorderly persons on Sundays, who molest and otherwise annoy females passing along the Highways of this Parish, and who also play at marbles and other unlawful games thereon, to the great Nuisance of the Public.

Now we do Hereby Give Notice,

that all persons found so offending *will be punished with the utmost severity of the Law.*

W. NORRIS FRANKLYN, } Churchwardens.
FRANCIS WELLS,

WARNHAM, 18th May, 1850.

Kennett and Breads, Printers, Bookbinders, Stationers, &c., West Street, Horsham.

47 *A notice posted by the churchwardens of Warnham parish threatening legal action against anyone causing a nuisance on the Sabbath.*

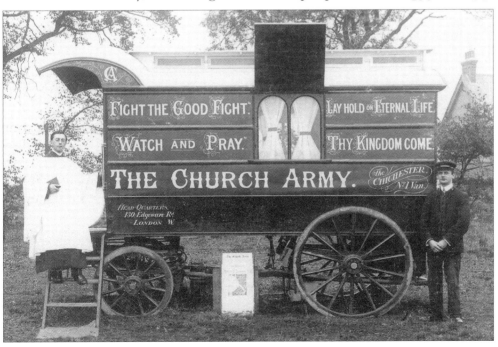

48 *Both the 'Lord's Day Observance Society' and the 'Church Army' (1904) were active in 'fighting the good fight' against the evil of drink, the former through exhibitions and the latter through a travelling wagon.*

49 *The imposing St Francis Lunatic Asylum, Haywards Heath opened on 25 July 1859 to serve West and East Sussex.*

and the reluctance of neighbouring counties to bail them out forced the county's hand and led to the construction of St Francis Lunatic Asylum in Haywards Heath. Increases in the numbers requiring treatment and more stringent requirements laid down by successive governments led to the opening of additional provision in East and West Sussex towards the end of the century. Graylingwell Hospital was built on the land of Graylingwell Farm, on the northern edge of Chichester in 1898, on a similarly elevated south-facing site.

The pressure on places provoked applications from entrepreneurs to open 'private' lunatic asylums. An application to open one for 35 patients at Craigweil House in Bognor Regis in 1875 led to opposition from local residents. After inspecting the premises the Report of the Commissioners of Lunacy concluded:

> it is well suited for convalescent patients and those of a quiet and orderly habit and demeanour. But in neither (House nor Lodge) are the arrangements fit for the reception of patients subject to maniacal excitement and violence, or for those having suicidal propensities, and we are of the opinion that if the Justices grant the Licence the two classes of patients just named should be specially excluded, by Endorsement on the Licence, from admission.

The petition from Bognor residents against granting the licence was signed by the leading citizens including the Fletchers, lords of the manor. Their reasons ranged from technical irregularities (insufficient period of notice, etc.) to the impact on the environment and neighbourhood, and the fact that despite a previous refusal of a licence the premises were already being used as an asylum in defiance of the decision of the Commissioners of Lunacy and the Justices:

A small, quiet watering place whose prospects depend solely on its visitors being enabled to allow their families and children to walk about unattended without fear of molestation from anyone … inmates have been allowed to wander about without proper supervision showing how detrimental and serious it would be to the neighbourhood if granted a permanent and general Licence … it will deter people who have resorted to that place for quiet and retirement from continuing to visit it.

50 *Graylingwell Hospital, Chichester opened as the Lunatic Asylum for West Sussex in 1897.*

This case might well have taken place today, suggesting that attitudes towards 'territory' have barely changed over the last 125 years or so.

Sea Shanties

In the 1920s and 1930s a rash of shanty towns pockmarked the West Sussex coastline. Enterprising families colonised the shingle ridges faster than the invading sea kale. Day trips to the seaside had opened their eyes to the possibilities of longer stays offered by unprotected beaches. All they needed was somewhere to stay and something to stay in. At first they pitched their tents on the shingle and bought provisions from nearby farms. But the attractions of the open air and proximity to the beach were outweighed by the uncomfortable beds. They overcame this drawback by buying redundant railway carriages and transporting them on lorries to their final resting place. It was this innovation which was imitated all along the coast from Shoreham to the Witterings.

The squatters levelled out a stretch of pebbles to house the railway carriage and gradually extended and disguised its origin with a bewildering array of wooden structures. In a relatively short time a shanty town of bungalows based on railway carriages sprung up at intervals along the shore. The individual make-overs gave, depending on your viewpoint, an attractive 'picturesque raffish' appearance to the area or that of an ugly rocky horror show.

51 *The destructive fire which consumed Sainsbury's superstore on the edge of Chichester on 16 December 1993 caused billowing smoke across the road. Its origin is still a matter of conjecture. The company blamed the architects for a 'design fault' but locals cite the construction of 'diabolical' plastic on a metal frame built on a former rubbish dump discharging methane as a contributory factor.*

53 *One of 25 fire engines at Sainsbury's superstore. As the fire raged the 'plastic excrescence' melted, the intense heat producing toxic fumes. The new store opened nine months later at a cost of over £10 million.*

52 *Three West Sussex fire brigade hoists pouring water into Sainsbury's superstore in an effort to contain the blaze.*

Conservationists tried to prevent the incursion of a motley crew of unsightly shacks, but at a time when 'planning' controls were limited they were impotent to curb the tide of excess. When the planning system was introduced after the Second World War there were successive attempts to remove a 'negation of planning'. Privately praying that it would be washed away by a tidal wave, the planners set out to rid the coastline of this 'blot on the landscape'. Public enquiries failed to substantiate the official case for demolition and over time planners took the view that if you can't beat them join them, and approved measures to convert temporary structures into permanent homes. In some instances this meant removal and replacement by a new bungalow bearing no resemblance to its former incarnation, but in others the railway carriage was incorporated into a modern dwelling.

The exotic names given to the bungalows convey the philosophies of the owners. 'Shangri-La' and 'Utopia' live side by side with 'L'Estrange', 'The Limit' and 'The Outpost'. The late comedian Tony Hancock filmed episodes in Bognor Regis and may well have stolen his 'Railway Sidings' from the development at Pagham Beach which sits alongside 'The End of the Line'. The recent conversions and newer buildings have greater pretensions, being prefaced by 'Villa' and built in Spanish Colonial style, but they are a reminder of a more carefree era when people's ambitions were not curtailed by impediments and bureaucracy. The 'little man' was able to imitate the 'wealthy' by having a holiday home at the seaside, and buying into the health-giving qualities promoted in print by Dr Russell and others which had stimulated the growth of seaside resorts such as Brighton.

Three

PROTEST

The 1820s and 1830s were decades of Protest. The growing political consciousness amongst the rising middle class was matched by the involvement of the disenfranchised in the hustings and the movement towards electoral reform which resulted in the Reform Act 1832 and the disappearance of 'rotten boroughs'. The Act changed the electoral landscape of the country, redistributing seats from rural, county shires to the hitherto unrepresented industrialising cities, and it expanded the franchise.

In a rural county such as West Sussex protests were largely focused on agriculture and the Poor Law provisions, and urban protest movements such as Chartism were poorly supported. A meeting of about 150 labouring men armed with stout staves from surrounding villages and a few local tradesmen, held in the *Fountain Inn*, South Street, Chichester in 1839, was addressed by Delegate Richardson, 'who uttered the usual inflammatory language associated with Chartism but had nothing new to say'. The meeting was considered to have been a failure.

Other reforms in the 1830s included the abolition of all slavery in British territories (1834), the first Factory Inspectors Act (1834), the first state grant to the churches to build schools, and the Poor Law Amendment Act (1834). It was in this atmosphere of progressive reform that 18-year-old Victoria became Queen in 1837. The momentum for change had gathered pace since the end of the Napoleonic Wars and reached fruition in the 1830s, thus appeasing a society which was on the brink of erupting.

Swing High Swing Low

In the post Napoleonic Wars period, when economic conditions were harsh and the poor were desperate, reform was in the air. The Swing

54 *Sullington Tithe Barn, full to the rafters with tithe corn, was threatened by the 'Swing' rioters in 1830 until the Rector agreed to reduce the tithe by 25 per cent. His wife, writing from the adjoining rectory, told her mother that she was afraid the 'mob' would set light to the barn.*

Riots of 1830 have entered folklore because they touched the lives of most people. About 250 rioters were convicted, of whom 19 were executed, and over 500 transported to Van Diemens Land (Tasmania). The 'Swing Riots' smouldered in Kent for about two months before permeating East Sussex in a fortnight and then sweeping through West Sussex in less than a week *en route* to Hampshire.

On 13 November 1830 'Swing' letters were circulated in Horsham, and fires raged at Ashington and Watersfield. On 15 November it was reported that threshing machines had been destroyed at Bersted, Bognor, Felpham and Yapton. On the same day the activities of the rioters alarmed the Mayor of Arundel so much that he enlisted 300 special constables to patrol the borough. Trouble was averted but only at the expense of the surrounding rural neighbourhood. On 16 November a massive fire at Old Place, Angmering consumed a wheat rick and two barns. Violent protest was the last resort of impotent poor tenants unable to express their anger through the ballot box or other democratic means.

Horsham, as an important market town, was an obvious target for the labourers to seek redress of their grievances. It was a centre of Radicalism, 'a hot-bed of sedition' according to one magistrate, where, on 19 November, a riotous vestry meeting was held in the parish church. A contemporary eye-witness reported that:

> ... early in the morning a large party assembled and strengthened their number by *forcing* people of every description to join them, and at 3 o'clock they went in an immense body to the church, where they insisted on being heard by Mr Simpson (Rector) and the major landowners.

All these gentlemen were stationed at the altar to receive the demands of this lawless multitude, who occupied every tenable place within the walls, and by their shouts and threatening language shewing their total disregard for the sanctity of the place. I am ashamed to say the farmers encouraged the labouring classes to be paid 2s. 6d. per day, while they called for their rents and tithes to be reduced by half.

Mr Simpson in a proper manner gave an account of the living and after shewing he did not clear more than £400 p.a. promised to meet the farmers and labourers to see what could be done. Mr Hurst (owner of the Great Tithes) had escaped as he feared blood would be shed. The doors were shut until the demands were met; no lights were allowed, the iron railings that surrounds the monuments torn up, and the sacred boundary between the chancel and the altar overleaped before he would yield. At last the points were conceded without personal injury.

The church is much disfigured. Money was afterwards demanded at various houses for refurbishment, and if not obtained with ease the windows were broken. Today the Mob is gone to Shipley and Rusper.

Chichester, another major market town, also became a focus of attention. On market day over 1,000 labourers gathered to confront the justices and principal farmers, who promised to remove their grievances. On 17 November 'a desperate gang' moved westwards breaking machines at Fishbourne, Bosham, Funtington, Westbourne, Chithurst and Rogate, and obtaining food, beer and money from householders by menace, threats and intimidation.

A letter from Charlotte Palmer, wife of the Rev. George Palmer, rector of Sullington, to her mother on 23 November 1830 indicates one of the rioters' principal grievances and the concessions made by the clergy. It also reveals the disruption to everyday life and the fear that stalked the community, forcing it to mount 24-hour vigils to combat the threat of violence:

I sit down to fulfil my promise of letting you know how matters have been settled with regard to the tythes which it was thought advisable to arrange yesterday instead of today as we were informed that if the farmers were satisfied we would not be visited by the mob. This has proved to be the case for Mr Palmer having taken off 15 per cent the farmers condescended to express themselves just satisfied and agreed to prevent the people paying us a visit. We may consider ourselves lucky in getting off so easily for Mr Wells of Wiston took off 30 per cent, Mr Woodward deducted half and many 25 per cent: however it is very vexatious to be obliged to give up any when we are quite sure that in many instances we did not receive as much as we ought to, in fact it is nothing more than robbery.

On Sunday morning a fire took place at a farm three miles off belonging to Mr Arkale at Findon, it blazed frightfully, three men were seen running away with crape on their faces but unfortunately they escaped; at this time two men came up to a rick of Mr Agate near us but two of his watchers fired at them and I am sorry to say that they escaped. Tonight all is quiet but I assure you that the situation is by no means enviable because after dark we are constantly looking out for fires and are afraid to go to bed until 12 or one o'clock. Mr Austin is in terrible alarm for he has an immense quantity of wheat, much of it tythe, and he has to watch it night and day and buckets of water are always in readiness. Mr Healy also has his premises constantly watched.

We see little or nothing of our neighbours for all visiting is suspended and people do not like to have visitors. I was saying this evening that I had been looking forward to enjoying the long winter evenings instead of which I heartily wish them over and as to opening the piano and attempting to play or sing I could not do it on any account.

One particular episode demonstrates that alongside the uncompromising mobs and rampaging gangs individuals were also protesting. George Olliver had bought Homestead Farm in East Preston in 1812. He attended church regularly and walked along a footpath which passed a cottage where Edmund Bushby, a 26-year-old local, unmarried labourer lodged. Exactly 400 yards from the cottage, measured by John Slater the overseer, stood a rick belonging to Olliver waiting to be threshed. Threshing by flail was one of the few winter occupations for farm labourers on subsistence wages of 10s. to 12s. a week, barely enough to buy bread for a family.

Olliver considered himself a progressive farmer and had purchased a new threshing machine, thereby posing a direct threat to one of the few sources of winter income. He used it as a bargaining tool, squeezing the amount he paid to his labourers down to 4s. a week. Bushby refused to accept such a derisory amount and insisted he was paid the 'Swing' rate of 14s.

When Olliver passed the cottage on his way home from church four days later Bushby confronted him again with his demand for the 'Swing' rate. Olliver refused to acquiesce and told him if he did not accept the rate offered he would have no work at all, even from the magistrate (poor law work). Bushby replied that if he was not given work by day he would 'work o' night'. Within 15 minutes the rick was alight.

56 *James Gillray's (1757-1815) gallows humour at the expense of the 'Swing' rioters. The wig, black hat and noose denote the price to be paid for burning the ricks in the background.*

It didn't take much intelligence to pin the crime on Bushby: he had taken a tinder box from his landlady and was publicly expressing the wish that Olliver was in the middle of the stack. On 21 December Olliver brought a prosecution against Bushby and in his summing up the judge admitted the evidence was only circumstantial as this was a 'deed of darkness'. Nevertheless, he concluded:

> Edward Bushby, you have been convicted on evidence the most clear and satisfactory, of setting fire to a rick, the property of Mr Olliver the prosecutor. Public justice and policy require that you should be made an example of. You must prepare to die; your days are numbered and few.

On New Year's Day 1831 he was executed in Horsham Gaol and buried, by his brothers, in an unmarked grave in East Preston churchyard.

Local tradition insists he was innocent and he became a martyr, accepting the ultimate punishment to cover up for the real culprit, his landlord, James Burcher. This view was given credence by the hasty departure of the Burcher family from the village and their never being heard of again. Bushby was the only 'Swing' rioter executed in Sussex.

A Crime of Anonymity

In late 1834 parishes were preparing their responses to the Poor Law Amendment Act passed earlier in the year. It was a highly contentious issue. On Sunday morning 23 November an anonymous letter was found attached to the gate post of Mr George Amoore's farm at Flansham in the parish of Felpham. He became a Guardian of the Poor in the Westhampnett Union, giving some measure of his status in the district:

> Understand that Coote and Amoore was for the runners of loring (lowering) the pay and if Amoore taken you down as I understand he sed he sud I Had lave of work and Drive the Buggar out of the place I had destroy the Buggars stack and then I set the rascals house on fire and after you don with him go and serve Coote the same You see he can hire a fly to go to the Ball and then he will stop 1 shilling per wick to pay fort (for it).

The 'Black Act' 1723 had made it a crime to send an anonymous letter, or one with a fictitious name, 'demanding money, venison or other valuable thing'. In 1754 this was extended to anyone making threats to kill, burn a house, barn, stack of grain, hay or straw, and convicted offenders would be liable to execution. The death sentence for this offence was repealed in 1823 and a maximum sentence of transportation for life substituted. The Swing Riots had been marked by a series of letters signed by the mysterious 'Captain Swing' so it was a live issue at the time.

The poorer classes feared the 1834 Act would reduce their wages and the amount of poor relief to which they had been entitled. The letter was a clear threat to take retaliatory action if this happened and was, in effect, blackmail. In such cases employees were invariably the main suspects. On this occasion Mr Amoore suspected William Boiling, one of his labourers, and tricked him into signing his name despite strenuous denials that he could even write. Using the similarities between the signature and the letter, especially the letters W and B, as evidence, he had Boiling arrested, taken before Arundel Magistrates and committed for trial at Petworth Assizes.

Boiling was acquitted and discharged because, without handwriting experts, 'evidence to handwriting was in general most vague and unsatisfactory, and there was no subject on which men could be so easily deceived'. The letter was no idle threat and rick burning and arson continued well into the century, with over fifty instances in West Sussex in the 1850s.

Pennsylvania Here I Come

William Penn was born near the Tower of London on 14 October 1644, the son of Admiral Sir William and Margaret Penn. He was expelled from Christ Church, Oxford for nonconformity in 1661. He regularly attended Quaker meetings and in 1668 met Guilema Maria Pennington, who was 'in all respects a desirable woman – whether regard was had to her outward appearance, which wanted nothing to render her completely comely; or to the endowments of her mind, which were in every way extraordinary; or to her outward fortune which was fair'. They married at Chorleywood in 1672 and moved to the 360 acres Warminghurst Estate in 1676, where Penn lived like a country squire, inviting criticism for advocating a plain, simple lifestyle 'while he swims himself in wealth'. The family became members of the Shipley Meeting, an offshoot of the Monthly Meeting at Horsham.

Penn protested against the persecution of nonconformists. In early 1681 he was amongst 20 Quakers charged at the Court of Assizes in Horsham (the first Quaker town in Sussex), some of whom were imprisoned for refusing to take the Oath of Allegiance, non-attendance at church and not paying their tithes. In March 1681 he was charged at the Assize Court at East Grinstead with trespass and contempt against the statute for discovering and repression of Popish recusants. The charge was dropped when he proved he was not a Roman Catholic.

57 *The Blue Idol Quaker Meeting House, Coolham, an offshoot of the Horsham Meeting, which Penn and his family attended regularly.*

58 *The interior of the Blue Idol is typical of the simplicity of a Quaker Meeting House and contrasted with the grandeur of Penn's mansion at nearby Warminghurst.*

59 *William Penn signing the treaty with the Indians for the foundation of Pennsylvania, 1682.*

In 1684 he was charged at Arundel Quarter Sessions as a

factious and seditious person who doth frequently entertain and keep unlawful assembly in his dwelling house usually assembled to ye number of one to two hundred and sometimes more to the terror of ye King's liege people and in contempt of the King and his laws.

This charge was also withdrawn, giving rise to the suspicion that he had supporters in the right places.

Convinced that there was no hope of reform in England for those with a 'conscience', Penn petitioned the King's Council to grant him a tract of land on the Atlantic seaboard of America where he could establish a 'Commonwealth' permitting freedom of worship. The Council saw the opportunity to settle a large outstanding debt owing to his father so it readily acceded to his request.

It was at Warminghurst that Penn conceived and planned the foundation of Pennsylvania, and where he received the Charter, signed personally by the King, on 14 March 1681. Here too, on 6 May 1682, he drew up his 'Frame of Government' (or draft constitution) for his 'Holy Experiment' for a colony tolerant of 'Dissenters'. Between 1681-5 he sold half a million acres to over 500 'First Purchasers', including 25 from West Sussex, three of whom were his servants.

On 30 August 1682 he boarded the 284 ton *Welcome* at Deal, *en route* for North America. At Worthing he was joined by other members of the Shipley Meeting: John Songhurst, carpenter, his wife Mary and daughter Sarah from West Chiltington, John Barber, a farmer, and his wife Elizabeth from Shipley, Wm. Buckman, carpenter, and his wife Mary and daughters Sarah and Mary from Billingshurst, John Rowland, Priscilla his wife and Hannah Muggeridge their servant, and his brother Thos. Rowland, all from Billingshurst. They arrived in the Delaware (named after the De la Warr family, East Grinstead) estuary on 27 October and disembarked at Chester on 28 October. On the journey 30 of the 100 passengers died from smallpox.

After two years establishing the colony Penn returned to England. His wife, Guilema, died in 1693. He wrote that she was 'one in ten thousand, wise, chaste, humble, plain, modest, industrious, constant and undaunted'. In 1696 he married Hannah Callowhill, daughter of a wealthy Bristol merchant, with whom he had six children. They continued to live at Warminghurst although it was no longer his principal residence. He got increasingly into debt, was thrown into a debtor's prison and was forced to sell Warminghurst in 1707 for £6,033, plus £2,300 for timber and stock, to meet his debts. The purchaser, James Butler, demolished Warminghurst 'to get rid of all traces of the old Quaker'. In 1712 Penn suffered a series of strokes and was incapacitated until his death in 1718.

Despite his achievement in establishing the colony of Pennsylvania, his heart resided in West Sussex and in his will he 'bequeathed to my Friends that are the poor of West Sussex in the first place and then to other Friends 10,000 acres of land in Pennsylvania for a township'.

60 *The Quaker Burial Ground in the corner of the cemetery at Twineham was rented from a sympathetic rector in 1654. The last recorded of over sixty burials was in 1732, but the Quakers still conduct a meeting at the site every three years to preserve their 'peppercorn' rent.*

The Cokelers – Church of the Quivering Brethren

In 1861 John Sirgood accepted 'A Lawyer's Notice to a Shoemaker to Discontinue Religious Worship in His Dwelling House'. He was the leader of a nonconformist sect in the north of the county, known as the 'Cokelers' from their habit of drinking cocoa. It is difficult to conceive the hostility to nonconformity which drove it underground and persuaded many dissenters to emigrate to obtain religious tolerance and freedom.

The sect was based in Loxwood and Warnham and in each place established a self-supporting 'cooperative' community based on 'socialist' principles. Its focus was the chapel, with worship three times on Sunday and two evenings during the week. The building, which cost £150, was almost

puritan in its simplicity, eschewing even a cross or crucifix because Christ had risen. The form of service was simple, with the leader and his 'Stalwarts', men and women, sitting on a long bench at the front chanting memorised biblical extracts and initiating hymn singing. The 'followers' discussed the texts and joined in the singing. When someone 'got the joy' they would stand up and deliver their testimony, often becoming 'possessed' in the process, from which derives the reference to the 'Church of the Quivering Bretheren'.

61 *The 'Peculiar People' (Cokelers) often became possessed by the spirit and said they were 'dancing in aid of religion'. This habit earned them the title of the 'Quivering Bretheren'.*

Lives revolved around work. The sect had farms, bakeries, dairies and shops which they ran themselves, for themselves, excluding 'outsiders'. The stores were run on a 'combination' basis with a secretary and trustees, and the members were shareholders earning 'dividends'. There is some debate as to whether they were paid wages or whether transactions were conducted by barter or a system of tokens. They 'hogged' village trade, selling a wide range of goods. They employed 31 members in the Warnham store and 12 at Loxwood.

Their hymns embraced their beliefs and ideals:

> Christ's combination stores for me
> Where I can be well supplied
> Where I can one with bretheren be
> Where competition is defied ...
> But let us to each other prove
> All by each other enriching
> 'Tis love that do each brother move
> For all to gain by trading.

The members built their own cottages and made furniture in their own workshops. They had a pottery making domestic wares. The original bill for the Warnham chapel and associated cottages built in 1874 was £252 12s. 9d. Warnham stores traded from 1879 until 1948, when dwindling numbers meant it was no longer viable, but it was not sold by the society until the 1970s. At its peak there were upwards of 2,000 members.

It did not advocate 'entanglements', meaning marriage, but since morality was fundamental to their lifestyle there was no embargo, and adherents were married in parish churches or in the presence of a registrar. John Sirgood, the founder, was married. He died in 1885 and was buried in

Loxwood. Members wore dark clothes and the women wore black dresses and poke bonnets similar to the Amish people in Pennsylvania.

The 'Cokelers' were honest, industrious, temperate, clean living people who integrated harmoniously in a close-knit community. Their alternative title, 'The Society of Dependents', sums up their dependence on each other and their communal reliance on the 'love of God'.

Richard Cobden, Agitator

Richard Cobden was born in 1804 in Dunford, near Heyshott, where he lived with his ten brothers and sisters on their grandfather's farm. When his grandfather died in 1809 his father bought a smaller farm at Guillards Oak, nearer Midhurst. The family suffered a series of misfortunes and the farm was sold and the children given homes by relatives. Richard moved to Yorkshire and after a stint as a clerk with a calico merchant in London went to Lancashire where he became a successful textile manufacturer.

62 *The inscription at the base of the obelisk summarises Cobden's ideals – Free Trade, Peace, Goodwill among Nations.*

At the age of 37 Cobden was elected a Member of Parliament for Rochdale and became a passionate advocate of Free Trade. After eight years of campaigning in conjunction with John Bright, the Corn Laws were repealed and the lot of the poorer classes made a little easier. He refused a knighthood and Cabinet position to continue as a back bencher championing the cause of the deprived and oppressed. The formation of the Anti-Corn Law League in 1839 was the catalyst for the emergence of the British middle class. It created a broad-based commercially-minded opposition to the landed aristocracy and brought together those elements which bridged the gap between rich and poor.

In 1847 he bought his birthplace and rebuilt it to house his young family. He found it a refuge from Westminster and returned there as often as possible. It grew on his wife, Kate, who persuaded him to give up their London home and make Dunford their main residence. The old farmhouse was replaced by a larger building. It was expected to be finished by Christmas 1853 but work was delayed. Cobden settled his family in a temporary home in Bognor. In order to supervise the building, 'Kate drove him in his carriage to the Duke of Richmond's park from where he would trudge over Goodwood Down and the unenclosed country beyond until he reached his own domain'.

One of the first visitors was his fellow M.P. and campaigner, John Bright, who observed that it was 'a nice house with a pleasing prospect from the windows and the lawn'. The two men enjoyed rides over the Downs, discussing the injustices which they agitated to put right. The list from Free Schooling to Universal Suffrage was in advance of its time but remarkably prescient.

Travelling the country, as well as the regular journeys from Dunford to London and London to Rochdale, took a toll on Cobden's health. Towards the end of November 1864 he visited Rochdale for what was to be his last public appearance. 'It was to be an enormous assemblage, I never saw so many people on one floor under one roof', with people 'standing in the outside alleys.' The exertions of that evening were too much for Cobden, who arrived home 'completely upset in every way from top to toe'. (Wendy Hinde, *Richard Cobden: A Victorian Outsider*, Yale University Press, 1987.) He was unable to leave his bedroom for a fortnight and did not really recover. On 2 April 1865 he died from broncho-pneumonia.

Cobden was buried in West Lavington churchyard beneath his beloved South Downs. A special train, with more than twenty carriages, brought hundreds of mourners from Waterloo to Midhurst, including M.P.s and deputations from the northern textile towns. His coffin was borne by 12 of his closest political friends and allies, including Bright and Gladstone. The warmth of the sunshine 'seemed to fight against the sorrow of the day'. The *Daily Telegraph* praised his great achievement in putting untaxed bread onto the poor man's table against all the odds, while other commentators highlighted his power to attract crowds and use the appropriate words to get his message across. *Punch* paid him the tribute of a 16-stanza poem devoted entirely to the repeal of the Corn Laws.

Although people did not always agree with Cobden they respected him as a man of principle and integrity who possessed a sincere conviction that the causes he promoted were for the good of the country and not for self interest or personal advancement. His single mindedness and inflexibility, and reluctance to compromise, prevented him reaching high rank, but his persuasive oratory, charm and ability to survive harsh battles with political rivals without bitterness and rancour, as well as the implementation of his life's work on the franchise and schooling soon after his death, ensure his permanent prominence as a politician of repute.

In 1930 a memorial tablet was unveiled in Heyshott church by Mrs Fisher Unwin, Cobden's only surviving child, Phillip Bright, son of John Bright, and Mr Henry Gladstone, the sole surviving son of William Gladstone, a fitting tribute from his closest allies. A stone obelisk at Pendean, on the road to Dunford, stands as a monument to his achievements:

FREE TRADE

PEACE

GOODWILL AMONG NATIONS

When Percy met Portia

Percy Bysshe Shelley, the poet, quarrelled with his father, who disowned and disinherited him. He returned periodically to his birthplace and home, Field Place, Warnham, usually when he was hard up, but he lived independently of the family.

The daughters of his uncle, Captain Pinfold, attended a school at Hurstpierpoint (in the house now called 'Abberton') run by Miss Elizabeth Hitchener, a young woman of modest means and dubious background (her father was reputed to have been a smuggler). She was respected for her independent, liberal, intellectual views and her achievements as a teacher. She was a striking figure, tall, raven-haired, dark-eyed, self-possessed and articulate. Her radical ideas derived from Thomas Paine and William Godwin.

Shelley met Elizabeth Hitchener through Captain Pinfold and the pair immediately established an extraordinary intellectual rapport, discussing religion and philosophy for hours. Shelley bombarded her with the latest literature on education, particularly that which advocated poetry as 'the most powerful means of instructing youth'. The friendship developed into a lengthy correspondence between June 1811 and June 1812 which became a testing ground for his philosophical and political theories. In a relatively short time she escalated from friend and correspondent to confidante and, finally, soulmate.

63 *A portrait of Percy Bysshe Shelley, the poet and revolutionary, as a young man.*

64 *A 1912 photograph of Cowdray House, Midhurst – an Elizabethan mansion destroyed by fire on 24 September 1793.*

65 *Abberton House, Hurstpierpoint where Elizabeth Hitchener established her school and acquired a deserved reputation for her enlightened methods and principles.*

66 *Idehurst House, Kirdford built by Thomas Strudwick in the 17th century, using local greensand and Horsham slates for the roof, with the proceeds of the glass industry and cider making in the Weald.*

Elizabeth Hitchener was conscious of the social chasm between them but was reassured by Shelley's sweeping condemnation of such distinctions. She was flattered by his attentions and treatment of her as his equal, and was half convinced that Shelley was in love with her. She was somewhat naive and accepted his arguments at face value, unaware that he had a private political agenda. Shelley had been sent down from Oxford because of a subversive treatise on atheism. He attributed the ills of society to the triumvirate of Religion, Monarchy and Aristocracy, and wrote extensively to Elizabeth on the subject. He asked her to join him and his wife (he had married hurriedly) and friends in founding an egalitarian community, where they could practise the principles he was expounding.

Matters took a sinister turn when a package of subversive material he had sent Elizabeth from Dublin was opened by the authorities because he had underpaid. The contents, in particular a 'Declaration of [working-class] Rights', were 'inflammatory' and of 'a militant tendency so dangerous to the government' that the Home Office was alerted. An agent was assigned to watch Shelley and monitor his 'connection' with Miss Hitchener.

Shelley resurrected the idea of the commune and invited Elizabeth, or Portia as she was now called, to join them at Nantgwillt. She was reluctant, as people in Sussex 'were talking' and Captain Pinfold and her father opposed it. The spectre of a 'sexual scandal' (Shelley's morals were now common knowledge) was sufficient deterrent. But Shelley dismissed Pinford and her father as 'vipers' and was determined that she should join his 'little circle' in her own right and not as the 'mistress' which the 'village gossips' whispered about. The rumours grew as their letters were intercepted and opened and the grapevine discussed the contents. He pleaded with her to liberate herself from her 'governors', which she eventually did, joining Shelley in Lynmouth. Elizabeth, or Bessy as she

was now known in Shelley's circle, tall, thin, writing, talking and laughing all day, reinvigorated Shelley to disseminate his propaganda.

The change from Portia to Bessy was, however, indicative of a lessening in affection towards her, especially on the part of Shelley's wife, who, jealous of the hold on her husband, resolved that Elizabeth could no longer be a member of the group. The 'showdown' occurred before they left once again for Wales. Elizabeth returned to Hurstpierpoint, where she was to be paid to 'work for the cause'. As Shelley's 'cast off' she was the object of ridicule and scandal. The lady scorned wrought vengeance in a succession of vitriolic letters threatening to denounce Shelley to the government, who referred to her as our 'Brown Demon', 'an artful, superficial, ugly beast of a woman' whose 'reputation is gone, health ruined, and peace of mind destroyed by my barbarity'.

Although embarrassed and poor, Elizabeth Hitchener's resolute spirit overcame rejection. She travelled abroad, met an Austrian officer, and returned to run a successful school in Edmonton until her death in 1822, the same year as Shelley's. She considered the time spent with him with fondness yet regret. A mutual physical as well as mental attraction between the subversive son of a baronet and the daughter of a smuggler and publican were never enough to overcome the insecurity and unrealistic ambitions of Shelley's flawed character.

Emigration

Poverty was widespread in the 1850s, subsistence wages for agricultural labourers were around 12s. a week, and in the countryside there were very few opportunities to escape its grip. Many were homeless and forced to live rough in barns, cart sheds, hovels and the open air. A few committed suicide, but William Dearing 'slit his throat from ear to ear with a pocket-knife' and survived! In Sutton paupers were treated like animals. They were yoked to carts to move stones from quarries to roads for breaking up by gangs of peasants supervised by an 'overseer'. The limited extent of their lives is summed up in this 'ditty' discovered in Lodsworth:

> Bread when we're hungry
> Beer when we're dry
> Bed when we're weary,
> Heaven when we die!

The workhouses, known disparagingly as 'pauper palaces', were their sole refuge. Their size and appearance was planned to intimidate and terrorise the able-bodied and deter the idle, but they provided a one-stop social service supplying shelter, food (even if it was a repetitive basic diet), clothes (even if it was a distinctive uniform), work (even if it was menial and back-breaking such as crushing bones), education and medical care. The regimes were harsh and monotonous, segregation by age and sex splitting up families, but

EMIGRATION
TO
SOUTH AUSTRALIA

Her Majesty's Colonization Commissioners having determined to dispatch in the
course of a few weeks a large number of Emigrants, all eligible persons may obtain, by
making an IMMEDIATE application, a

FREE PASSAGE!

The classes of persons now in requisition are
Agricultural Laborers,
SHEPHERDS, CARPENTERS
BLACKSMITHS
AND
STONE MASONS
And all Persons connected with Building.

Application to be made to

67 *Emigration to South Australia, under the auspices of the Petworth Emigration Committee, was sponsored by the 3rd Earl of Egremont.*

by themselves they catered for the poor and vulnerable, which duty 150 years later is shared amongst numerous agencies.

Conditions, restrictions and personal circumstances made it difficult to travel long distances so that 80-90 per cent of people lived in the parishes in which they were born or in adjacent ones. Few moved to London or the industrialising northern towns, but many paupers thought the grass might be greener on the other side of the world. They believed that emigration held out their best hope of release from destitution.

Between 1830 and 1850 the Petworth Emigration Committee, bankrolled by the 3rd Earl of Egremont (d.1837) and his successor, his nephew Colonel George Wyndham, 1st Baron Leconfield, and masterminded by the Rev. Thomas Sockett, rector of Petworth, and the churchwardens, sponsored more than 1,800 emigrants to York (now Toronto), Canada and 600 to the first non-convict Crown Colony of South Australia, a 100-days' journey under sail in a 300-tons 'brig'. The committee convinced applicants that 'emigration was not a banishment but only a removal from one part of the British Empire where there was no work to another more fertile, healthful and delightful portion where there is plentiful work to be performed'.

Many believed that emigration 'removed vicious characters steeped in vice and habitual pauperism who preferred expatriation to honest endeavour at home', but the spin doctors of the day claimed that emigrants were of 'a respectable class of mechanics and peasantry', the deserving poor. Their departure certainly relieved population pressure in Petworth and neighbouring parishes, eased the financial burden on Colonel Wyndham and other landowners, and cut parish rates. It paid to assist emigration because it saved the cost of keeping paupers on parish relief in Britain and each emigrant was a £10 bonus to the British economy as a prospective consumer.

In the late 1830s and the early 1840s Chichester emigrants helped to found Adelaide, the capital of South Australia. John Barton Hack, a member of the family which launched the Chichester Bank in East Street in 1809 and sold the business to Barclays in 1900 for 2,000 £20 shares, emigrated from Graylingwell Farm, Chichester. He served on the committee that named the streets in Adelaide, including Barton Street, Sussex Gardens and East, West, South and North Pallant among them. He travelled as a government subsidised emigrant recruited by his brother-in-law, Henry Watson of South Street, Chichester, the local agent for the Colonisation Commissioners who received 1s. for each emigrant who turned out to be a good egg.

By the 1850s emigration had achieved its objective, population had peaked in West Sussex and a long period of decline had begun. Rural losses were not balanced by the pockets of modest population growth in the market towns and along the coast. The transition from small-scale parish-based administration towards larger-scale centralised authority was well under way. Soon the functions combined in the workhouses would be disbursed as a series of Acts in the late 19th century, such as the 1870 Education Act, set the wheels in motion for universal school provision and attendance, established embryo local authorities, built lunatic asylums and improved health through introducing sanitation measures and hygienic water supplies. The petty 'feudal kingdoms' of the aristocracy were being invaded and undermined on political, administrative and economic fronts.

68 The plaque commemorating the founding of the Chichester Bank by the Hack family in 1809 is outside Barclay's Bank, East Street, Chichester, to whom the family sold the business for 2,000 £20 shares in 1900.

69 A list of 'Necessaries' for emigration to Upper Canada.

Scandal in the Workhouse

At local level, workhouse administration was punctuated by scandals, usually involving illegal 'connections' between different classes of paupers

---

List of Necessaries for Emigrants to UPPER CANADA.

Families should take their	*Single Men must have*
Bedding.	A Bed or Mattress.
Blankets.	Metal Plate or wooden Trencher.
Sheets, &c.	Some kind of Metal Cup or Mug.
Pewter Plates or wooden Trenchers.	Knife, Fork and Spoon.
Knives and Forks and Spoons.	
Metal Cups and Mugs.	
Tea Kettles and Saucepans.	*All, or any of which, may be procured at Portsmouth, if the Parties arrive there unprovided.*
Working Tools of all descriptions.	
(A large tin Can or watering pot would be useful)	

Besides various other portable Articles in domestic use (especially of metal) according as Families may be provided. A Cask, not exceeding the size of a Hogshead or 60 Gallons, affords an excellent and dry case, for packing such Articles as are not likely to be wanted 'till the end of the voyage. All packages should be marked with the Owner's name, in large Letters. ⟶ hundred weight *One* of Luggage is allowed to be taken by each Individual above 14 years of age.

The following is the lowest outfit recommended to Parishes for their Laborers.

A Fur Cap.	Two Jersey Frocks.
A warm great Coat.	Four Shirts.
A Flushing Jacket and Trowsers.	Four pairs Stockings.
A Duck Frock and Trowsers.	Three pairs Shoes.
A canvas Frock & two pairs of Trowsers.	A Bible and Prayer Book.

Women in the same proportion, especially a *warm Cloak.*

All the above may be purchased at Petworth.

It is also a matter of great importance, that Emigrants should take with them a good Character, (if they should have the happiness to possess one,) fairly written and well attested, also Copies of Marriage or Baptismal Registers, or any other Certificates or Papers likely to be useful; the whole to be inclosed in a small Tin Case.

J. Phillips, Printer, Petworth.

70 Petworth House of Correction.

and not infrequently between the officers and inmates. Such a scandal occurred in Petworth Workhouse in 1841.

Accusations of improper behaviour were made against the 'Master', Mr John Penfold. The demands on the Masters were enormous and unrealistic. They were uneducated, overworked, underpaid and inadequately supervised, so it is little wonder that 'irregularities' were common and that they abused their authority. Complaints emanating from the paupers was considered unreliable and their 'evidence' was treated with suspicion; nevertheless, they were heard.

Undue familiarity with female paupers was against the rules. The case was heard by Mr Tufnell, the Assistant Poor Law Commissioner for East Sussex. He heard statements from the witnesses and Mr Daintrey, a Solicitor and Secretary of the Petworth Poor Law Guardians, cross-examined them:

> Emma Lucas had come from London 6 years previously and had been in the workhouse ever since. She delivered a male child on 16th February. She had left the workhouse in June when she was in the family way again and had another child in Wisborough Green workhouse. She claimed that Penfold was the father of both children. He had asked her to leave soon after he got her into trouble and gave her 17s. two or three times. She told Daintrey that noone else had given her money and that she had resisted his advances 'in the larder'. He persisted and wanted 'to have connection with me'. I refused but he laid hold of me and took liberty with me.
>
> Mary Ann Dummer claimed that Penfold 'put his hands up my clothes and also made me put my hands in his breeches. Other nights when mistress was in bed he used to put his hands up our clothes. He told us not to tell or else he would be cross with us. Once I caught Master and Emma Lucas in the storeroom and another time in the bedroom with her clothes rumpled.'
>
> Priscilla Lucas, aged 17, confirmed the pattern. 'Penfold used to put his hands up our clothes and put our hands in his trousers. Master first took liberties with me about four months ago and gave me two sixpences and four pence. He told us if we told we would have no holidays. The rumpling of Lucas's clothes was talked of downstairs.

Hannah Henley went into the workhouse the previous October and Penfold put his hands up her petticoat in the winter. She said she did not resist him or complain. 'When I objected he gave me 1s. twice not to say anything about.' Hannah boasted to the others that she had the power of turning her Master on at half an hours notice. Sarah Grant said, 'I never asked how only said ooh is that right Hannah.'

Mary Ann Elliot, 16 years, claimed that as she was coming down the garret stairs she had seen Mr Hale, the Medical Officer, give Emma Lucas 1s. 6d. 'I saw them before the money was given go into the lying in room together and shut the door.'

On 24 April 1841 Mr Tufnell reported to the Poor Law Commission in London that he had attended the Petworth Board 'yesterday' and adjudicated as follows:

> The evidence is rather conflicting, but the Guardians determined that although they did not consider the matter fully proved, yet, sufficient came out in the evidence to make them doubt whether he might have been guilty of some inappropriateness – Mr Penfold should be required to send in his resignation. I did not go to this extent and knowing the character of Workhouse witnesses I did not give full credit to their assertions. However I think enough was proved to throw considerable suspicion on his conduct and it is altogether better that he should resign his situation.

Mr and Mrs Penfold resigned on 24 May. As soon as the Petworth Board of Guardians received confirmation from the Poor Law Commission they appointed Mr Hall (29 years), Deputy Keeper of the Petworth House of Correction, and his wife Harriet (35 years) to be Governor and Matron of Petworth Workhouse at a combined salary of £60 p.a. (compared with the Medical Officer's remuneration of £100 p.a.). They had two children. Harriet signed the contract with X her mark.

The purpose of workhouses was partly to 'reform the undisciplined impulses of paupers, criminals and delinquents' as part of the various campaigns of moral regulation instituted during the 19th century. In the context this episode epitomised the struggle for the 'riff-raff' to be taken seriously by the powerful local elites and provided a forum for their objections to abuse, bribery and even rape to be considered. The fact that only three per cent of workhouse governors were dismissed and pressure exerted on another ten per cent to resign illustrates that it was a small beginning, but the evidence, as at Petworth, had to be convincing.

Damp Squibs

The Reform Act 1832 removed or reduced the representation of Members of Parliament elected by 'rotten boroughs', and extended the franchise to those owning property worth £10 a year or more. It was intended to end the practice of patronage, whereby seats were in the gift of the leading aristocratic families or major landowners. The fact that it failed in its prime objective, as the local oligarchy endured, is a comment on the persistence of deferential habits and behaviour towards authority as much as on their power and influence.

"FARMER TEE."

[To the tune of "Farmer Giles."]

Now, I've come down from Rudgwick—my name's Farmer Tee ;
If you read the papers you've all heard of me.
To study political questions I try,
For a regular Radical farmer am I.

CHORUS :
Ri-tooral ri-tooral ri-tooral ri-tay,
You'll pardon my singing, I'm feeling so gay,
But the Liberal Party's a-having its day—
Ri-tooral ri-tooral ri-tooral ri-tay.

I'm only a plain man as works on the land,
But the good of Protection I can't understand.
Suppose all our wheat comes across the blue sea—
I can't see as that'll be much use to me.

Ri-tooral ri-tooral ri-tooral ri-tay,
What rubbish these Tariff Retormers do say !
Encourage the Colonies to ruin me—eh ?
Ri-tooral ri-tooral ri-tooral ri-tay.

We've smart men in Sussex, for *we* can afford
To have for our member a noble young lord.
His notions are funny and don't do no harm—
But the best of the lot was his strawberry-farm !

Ri-tooral ri-tooral ri-tooral ri-tay,
We misses his joking since he went away,
But perhaps he'll come back with some fresh jokes
some day !
Ri-tooral ri-tooral ri-tooral ri-tay.

And when he comes back from his holiday trip
He'll find a new war-cry on every lip.
And it's " Freedom for all from the power of the Lords,
Let's put 'em on show down at Madame Tussaud's ! "

Ri-tooral ri-tooral ri-tooral ri-tay,
We want to get on, but they stand in the way,
They'll find they've got notice to quit some fine day,
Ri-tooral ri-tooral ri-tooral ri-tay.

Now Sussex wants leaders prepared for the fight,
(We've got the right sort on the platform to-night).
There are lots of young Liberals as keen as can be
To have a new member instead of Lord T.

Ri-tooral ri-tooral ri-tooral ri-tay,
I'm only a farmer as means what I say,
But with " *One man, one vote,*" we shall have our own
way.
Ri-tooral ri-tooral ri-tooral ri-tay.

D.W.T.

71 *A 'damp squib' – 'Farmer Tee' ridiculing Turnour's (Earl Winterton's) candidacy in a 19th-century election.*

It was not until 1859 that the 'pocket borough' of Midhurst 'threw off the shackles of the Cowdray interest' and 'Midhurst men breathed free', when the electors rejected Hardy, a Banbury man and the nominee of Lord Egmont, and chose one of their own, W. Townley Mitford of Pitshill, Tillington, as M.P. to 'remove the badge of serfdom'. He was a magistrate and a 'gentleman of the highest character' whose election broke up the 'disreputable nomineeship' which had seen the electors 'handed from a Walpole to a Warren and a Warren to a Hardy'. As a local man living in the constituency, Mitford was more likely to represent their interests and 'not merely the wishes of a patron'.

It was a defining moment. The electors in Midhurst summoned up the courage to confront the local aristocrat who was also their employer and owner of many of their homes. Yet, nearly 30 years after the passing of the Act, the Cowdray faction attempted to exercise its muscle and intimidate the voters. One voter, replying to an enquiry from the *West Sussex Gazette* as to how the election campaign was proceeding, informed the newspaper, 'Fust rate. Mr Mitford is sure to get in. But law there's something to come out. Aint they bin and put the screw on thats all.' The newspaper published a letter written to a voter, a former employee of the Cowdray Estate, by Lord Egmont's butler, James Seaton, nicknamed James Plush of the Big House, undertaking to reinstate him if he voted for the Lord's candidate in the 1859 General Election.

After being highly critical of such a blatant attempt at bribery and intimidation, the *West Sussex Gazette* published this 'Damp Squib' to 'the insinuating Lothario':

Oh James Thou seekst my love in vain,
Thou feckless, fickle valentine,
Why this change – this whining cry?
Excuse me Jeaves, its gone in my eye.
You'd have me sell my honest name
By promising the work again.
You first proved false – ah! Do not frown,
And now you seek a vote for Browne.
My word is given. To Mitford's cause I stick,
Indeed I shall Jeaves, like a jolly brick.

Captain Isemonger's Silver Dagger

Another of the great moral crusades in the 19th century was the abolition of slavery, led by Wilberforce and finally achieved in the British Empire in 1834 but not until 1865 in America, where it was eventually prohibited by a constitutional amendment imposed at the end of the Civil War.

Captain Richard Isemonger's great, great, great granddaughter possesses an ornately fashioned dagger with a silver handle, reputedly the gift of a Moorish prince. How did it come into his possession and what is the connection between Littlehampton, where he was brought up, and the slave trade? Richard was born into a well-established shipbuilding family in Littlehampton in 1808, probably in River Road adjacent to the shipyards. By 1840 he was Master of the brig *Africanus* belonging to London merchants Forster and Smith.

Word of the capture of two London-based vessels and the slaughter or capture of their 11 crew reached Captain Isemonger, who was sailing along the West African coast. He had acquired an enviable reputation amongst the Moors as a firm but fair trader and he offered to exploit his relationship with them to negotiate the release of the prisoners. He knew the captives would be sold into slavery, as the Trazar Moors were notorious slave traders, but he also knew that they were formidable opponents and could be bought at a price. He proposed paying a ransom for the release of the prisoners, and the acceptable price of freedom was 330 bales of matting. He left with six of the prisoners, two being snatched back on departure because of a disagreement amongst the captors over the distribution of the ransom, and took them to the Gambia to be picked up by the next ship heading for England.

The authorities attempted to obtain the release of the five seamen remaining in the hands of the Moors without success so, despite the danger, Isemonger decided to go direct to 'King' Abdullah, the potentate who held sway over the area. His standing was such that they were released immediately and taken to a neighbouring island for collection. The captives returned to England in April 1845, 11 months after they had been captured.

72 *A 'brig' moored at Town Quay, Arundel in the 1880s. Silting, larger boats, a new 'cut' at the mouth of the River Arun, the arrival of the railways and the consequent loss of traditional imports such as coal led to the demise of Arundel as a port and the transfer of functions to Littlehampton at the mouth of the Arun.*

Isemonger presented his account to Acting-Governor Mantell at Bathurst, Sierra Leone, who advised him to present it to Her Majesty's Government on his return to England because of the amount involved. The claim, on behalf of his owners, for £313 10s. od. was met and Isemonger himself was given the derisory sum of £26 10s. od. for his exertions in rescuing the first six prisoners and the promise of a further £15 for the other five, if and when it was approved.

Isemonger's treatment was publicised in the newspapers and influential allies in the Army and Navy Club took up the case with Lord Aberdeen, the Foreign Secretary. Acid letters emphasised the fact that the seamen had been freed through the efforts of a private merchantman, not the British Government, and insisted he should be rewarded accordingly. After 12 months' correspondence between the Foreign Office and the Treasury, Captain Richard Isemonger was awarded the sum of £500 in recognition of his diplomacy, and Lord Aberdeen considered he was 'by no means overpaid'. He also received a Gold Medal, also in the possession of his great, great, great granddaughter, who emigrated to New Zealand.

This account emerged from the Slave Trade Correspondence of the Foreign Office in the Public Record Office. Unfortunately the source does not reveal the donor of the dagger, but is it too fanciful to attribute it to the royal treasure house of King Abdullah?

The Manor of Donnington

A number of West Sussex estates owed their existence and wealth to slavery. In 1800 George White married Francis Page, daughter of John Page, M.P. for Chichester, and became lord of the manor of Donnington. He inherited the manor from his father, John White, a plantation owner on the island of St Christopher (now St Kitts) in the West Indies who retired to Chichester and bought his servant, John Gray, a freehold cottage and piece of land in Pagham in recognition of the great care he had taken of him during several illnesses in St Christopher, where smallpox was endemic.

John White's last will and testament of 2 March 1775 is a revealing and intriguing insight into attitudes towards and relationships between the owner and his slaves on a sugar plantation at the time. White appears to have been a humane and caring owner yet that did not alter the status of slaves as mere chattels.

> … also chargeable with the payment of one annuity or yearly rent charge of £10 sterling apiece to two *mulatto* women named Sarah and Frances whom I made free before I left St Christopher to be paid annually during their respective lives and after my decease two negro girls each of about 16 years of age be purchased out of the rents and profits of my estate and one of them for the sole use and benefit of the said Frances and the other for Sarah as their respective property.
>
> … and I charge my estate with the further payment of an annual sum of £10 sterling apiece unto the beforenamed two *mulattos* Sarah and Frances during their respective lives over and above the annuity. And whereas by the Laws and Customs of the island of St Christopher Negroes and other stock commonly and successively used and workt with upon Plantation Estates thereof as freehold nature are considered as chattels only and unmoveable therefrom which if removed would greatly depreciate if not totally ruin such Plantations therefore to prevent such loss and inconvenience I direct that all negroes and other slaves mules cattle horses utensils and implements of every kind at the time of my death shall be considered as heirlooms and shall remain thereon for the benefit of my Plantation Estate and

73 *General Booth, the Salvation Army leader, arriving in Worthing in 1907.*

shall accordingly be possessed by the person or persons who become entitled to the possession of my said real Estate … I will and direct that my Slaves be at all times used with Humanity and Tenderness as the nature and intention of their business will admit and not be treated with any degree of cruelty and that all such slaves as are grown old in my service be well lookd after and fed and taken care of in a proper manner.

The survival of a yellowing account of the Estate shows the number and names of the slaves, the stock, the accommodation, and the equipment and its value. It also gives a picture of the traditional shingled and clapboard appearance of the buildings.

Another landowner who purchased his estate with the proceeds of plantations and slavery was John Henry of Blackdown, in the north of the county.

Reading the Riot Act in Worthing 1883

In 1902 General William Booth was invited to the Coronation of King Edward VII, and on 28 November 1905 George Bernard Shaw's *Major Barbara* had its premiere in London in the presence of Prime Minister Balfour. By the beginning of the 20th century the Salvation Army had become the respected organisation it is today. It had not always been the case.

Conditions in the urban areas in the late 19th century were ripe for organisations such as the Salvation Army to exploit the distress and preach their gospel of conversion. Frequently, the strident tone of the message and the tactics employed inflamed an already volatile situation.

In September 1883 the *Worthing Gazette* reported that 'The long threatened invasion by the fanatics of the Salvation Army has at last taken place'. Virtually simultaneously Captain Margetts had sent a telegram from Worthing to The Salvation Army H.Q.

> attacked yesterday; whole town moved; powerful morning meeting; drill good, fifty present; crowds in Market at ten; short, heavy firing; glorious march to hall; hall filled; good order; Great gathering; rough element, completely overwhelmed; closed meeting early. Hall packed at night; crowds outside; stormy meeting; many wounded. Glorious prospect; great victory near! Our King will reign! Hallelujah! Police rendered assistance.

The Salvation Army imitated the army with uniforms and ranks such as Sergeant, Lieutenant, Captain, Major, Brigadier and General. They used the language of organised violence and rallied their army of Christian soldiers under the banner of a magazine called *War Cry*.

The Salvation Army considered seaside resorts fertile recruiting grounds. By the time they turned their attention to Worthing they had already provoked trouble in sixty small towns in the south and west of the country. In Honiton and Weston-super-Mare a rival army of young men had confronted the salvationists and disturbances ensued. Known as 'The Skeleton Army' because they adopted the skull and crossbones as their logo, their name became synonymous with opponents of the Salvation Army. They were backed by supporters from a 'higher social position' who viewed the Salvation Army as subversive and a threat.

What began as 'youthful rowdies' baiting and interrupting meetings often ended up as riots. In extreme cases the Skeleton Army attacked the Salvation Army 'Barracks', causing mayhem. The prospect of confrontation attracted

74 *Damage caused by rioters in Worthing protesting against the activities of the Salvation Army in 1883.*

TOWN OF WORTHING
CAUTION.

WHEREAS

Divers Persons are continually collecting and taking large quantities of

BOULDERS

from the Sea Beach, and sending the same away by Railway and in Boats for the purpose of exportation to other parts of the Country, thereby seriously weakening the Sea Beach, and endangering the safety of the Esplanade in front of the Town.

Now I do hereby, in pursuance of **AN ORDER OF THE COMMISSIONERS OF THE TOWN**, give notice that if any person is found taking and sending away Boulders in Boats, or by Railway, or in any other manner for exportation, he will be prosecuted for the offence.

CHARLES HIDE,
SURVEYOR.

Worthing, January 14th, 1852.

Moore and Wilkins, Printers, Worthing.

75 *A poster ostensibly prohibiting the collection of boulders (pebbles) from Worthing beach for sale or export, but the intention was to deter their use as ammunition during periods of unrest.*

dissidents to swell the ranks and the peaceful sabbaths of genteel Worthing were turned into 'rowdy carnivals'. Rotten eggs were replaced by bricks and stones, the pebble beach providing an inexhaustible supply, and glass was broken. The police originally kept a low profile and the magistrates, unable to prevent the lawful Salvation Army 'marches', favoured the 'roughs' intent on disrupting them.

> Most noble Worthing magistrates,
> Whose judgements are sublime:
> To beat a policeman is a joke,
> But to beat a drum a crime.

Eventually pressure from local inhabitants forced the magistrates to act and three leaders of the 'mob' were imprisoned for a month with hard labour. Angry crowds of up to 4,000 people roamed the town seeking revenge. The magistrates summoned assistance from the police, special constables and a troop of Royal Irish Dragoons from Brighton. The crowd refused to disperse, there were injuries and, eventually, a fatality, so Colonel Wisden, chairman of the magistrates, read the Riot Act for the only time in Worthing's history. Skirmishes continued spasmodically for the rest of the year but ultimately order was restored and the Skeleton Army moved on.

Suffragettes and Suffragists

One of the strongest protest movements eventually resulted in the enfranchisement of women. There were two main associations campaigning for votes for women. The National Union of Women's Suffrage Societies (NUWSS), founded by Millicent Fawcett in 1897, were known as the Suffragists and the more militant Women's Social and Political Union (WSPU), founded by Emmeline Pankhurst and her daughters in 1903, were known as Suffragettes. Both had branches and supporters throughout the country.

In Worthing a branch of the NUWSS was established by Mrs Ellen Chapman, who in 1910 became the town's first female councillor. She organised coffee mornings and 'at homes' to advertise the cause. The WSPU went in for headline-catching rallies. In early 1913 they held one in the Kursaal (now Dome Cinema) to be addressed by Mrs Pankhurst, who failed to make it because she had been arrested for inciting the perpetrators of a bombing at a house where the Prime Minister, Lloyd George, was due to speak.

Several thousand people turned up for the meeting and the Kursaal was packed. Close associates of Mrs Pankhurst, including Mrs Israel Zangwill of

East Preston, were scheduled to speak. The audience included several young men the worse for drink whose sole object was to disrupt proceedings. Pepper bombs were thrown onto the stage and bugles played whenever someone rose to address the gathering. The meeting had to be abandoned and the suffragettes were forced to escape by the back door. They were accosted by the crowd and an attempt was made to duck two of them in the drinking trough outside the town hall. Subsequent meetings were also disrupted but local opinion distanced itself from the 'hooligans' and insisted on campaigners being given 'a fair hearing'.

Mrs Florence de Fonblanque, who lived at Duncton from 1913-49, organised the famous long march of the 'Brown Women', so called because of the working uniform, emerald green tie and cockades, which they wore from Edinburgh to London in October/November 1912. The march meandered from market town to market town, holding meetings and gathering signatures for 'Votes for Women in the present Session of Parliament'. By the time it arrived in London a van was required to transport the signatures from Camden Town underground station, where the marchers were joined by Suffrage Societies from all over London, including men, to descend on Downing Street. The crowd which greeted them in Trafalgar Square was so large the marchers had to hold five meetings simultaneously, with the principal speakers rotating between each. Mrs de Fonblanque was the star performer and her message to the crowd and Prime Minister Asquith was 'the country is with us'.

76 *Mrs Florence de Fonblanque's grave, Duncton.*

The march of the 'Brown Women' had a tremendous impact, generating huge publicity in the national newspapers which charted the enthusiastic welcome the marchers received *en route* and the extraordinary lengths they went to to canvass signatures. Florence de Fonblanque, the daughter of an Italian immigrant who married a French Comte and resided in the West Sussex countryside, deployed her acting skills and organisational ability to make an indelible impact on the suffragette movement in this country. She subsequently founded and led 'QUI VIVE CORPS' and her 'Pilgrimage' was imitated by the major players.

In July 1913 the NUWSS organised a march from Brighton to London, following the example set by the 'Brown Women'. They held meetings and provided entertainment at each town and village *en route* in order to recruit marchers. Their experience at Cuckfield mirrored that elsewhere: it poured

77 *Prime Minister Lloyd George addressing a suffragette meeting in Worthing.*

with rain, the meeting and entertainment had to be cancelled, only a few hardy souls braved the weather to watch the marchers, and even fewer 'bolder spirits' joined the march.

The suffragettes finally achieved their objective, but universal female suffrage was only granted in 1928. Their long and frequently violent struggle demonstrates the lengths that had to be taken to overturn, what, in retrospect, appears to have been an indefensible position.

Education, Education, Education

The 1902 Balfour Education Act meant the Church lost exclusive control of schools when responsibility for providing primary, secondary and further education was placed into the hands of local authorities. But what has been hailed as one of the three greatest legislative achievements of the 20th century did not meet with universal approval. A frequent opinion expressed at the time, which still has resonance today, was that 'Childhood looks likely to be made a serious business. If we are not careful it will become nothing but a time of training, tasks and tears. School Boards and school teachers in Board schools (non-church) need to learn that they cannot force brains. Nature will resent it.'

The Act impinged directly on families. A Barnham mother wrote to the headmaster:

> I want Emma at home but it seems you are going to do as you like with the children. I will send them to school for proper learning but not for such rubbish as to learn cooking. Emma says I have to pay a penny for a book but I have too many ways for my pennies and I will not give a penny for anything of the sort.

Parents objected to losing a helping hand to bring in the harvest or attend the local fox hunt, so a carrot and stick policy was adopted. District Attendance Officers, 'Whippers-in', were appointed to round up absentees, while incentives were offered to encourage attendance: cards were given for one week's perfect attendance, a certificate for a good annual attendance, a bronze medal for one year's perfect attendance and a solid silver watch for five years' perfect attendance.

In 1908 the Local Authority Education Boards became responsible for children's health. Medical inspections were conducted at 8, 12 and 15 years of age, which largely eliminated the epidemics that closed schools, although tuberculosis remained a problem. The eradication of contagious diseases and the steps taken to combat absenteeism improved school attendance.

Four

CRIME AND PUNISHMENT

At the end of the 18th century and beginning of the 19th century there was no police force, and in most places law and order was in the hands of untrained parish constables appointed annually by the parish vestry. Their origin goes back to the early medieval period and the manorial system and they were ill-equipped to meet the needs of an increasingly lawless Georgian England.

Land and property owners joined together to form prosecution societies to protect themselves and their properties and to convict culprits. They were a cross between self-help groups, insurance societies and vigilantes, setting out to catch, arrest and convict criminals. They believed their property was sacrosanct and trespass of any kind for any purpose was sacrilege.

Members of a Prosecuting Society had to pay an entrance fee and an annual subscription and augment the funds if they became too low. In Wisborough Green the entrance fee was half a guinea and the annual fee 5s. The fund was to remain at about £50 and was not allowed to go below £30. The costs determined the composition of the Society, restricting it to those who could afford to pay for protection and debarring farm labourers. The majority were male but in 1810 there were five female members.

The Society had an elaborate list of 'Articles' or rules, including these rewards for the discovery of offenders:

Wisborough Green
PROSECUTING SOCIETY,
Established MARCH 8th, 1792,
FOR RAISING A FUND TO PROSECUTE
Felons, Thieves, Receivers of Stolen Goods, &c.
AND FOR PAYING
REWARDS ON CONVICTION.

78 *Wisborough Green Prosecuting Society prospectus, 1792.*

5 Guineas
REWARD.

Henfield Prosecuting Society.

WHEREAS some evil disposed Person or Persons did in the Night of Saturday the 27th of February last, or early on Sunday Morning, wantonly or maliciously pull up and carry away a quantity of

BUSHES

from the Hedge in a Field in the occupation of *Mr. James Funnell*, at Henfield, and did also take and carry away certain **GATES** belonging to other *Members* of the said Society, and commit various other depredations.

A Reward of TWO GUINEAS will be given to any Person or Persons making discovery of the Offender or Offenders so that he or they may be Convicted thereof---The Reward to be paid immediately after Conviction by the Treasurer of the said Society.

Horsham,   *THOMAS COPPARD*,
1st March, 1836.   *Clerk.*

A further Reward of THREE GUINEAS will be given on Conviction as aforesaid, by me   *JAMES FUNNELL.*

Charles Hunt, Printer, West Street, Horsham.

79 *A reward offered by the Henfield Prosecuting Society.*

£5 for the conviction of anyone murdering a Society member, robbing or setting fire to one of their houses or robbing one of them on the highway.
£1 1s. od. for anyone stealing cattle, hop poles or similar.
10s. 6d. for anyone stealing wood, faggotts, coal, garden implements, etc.

It is interesting to observe that a life was valued the same as a robbery or a fire!

The Society met annually and elected a Clerk and a Treasurer. Decisions during the year were taken by the Clerk and seven members, who decided whether to proceed with a prosecution. By modern standards many of the offences were trivial. Most involved petty thefts of turnips from gardens, sacks of wheat off wagons, fish from White Brook, cheese and bacon from a storehouse, and a Mr Evasted's horses 'had something administered to them'. Complaints were received two or three times a year but in general Wisborough Green was law abiding.

Posters advertised rewards for information leading to convictions. The Wisborough Green Society offered a £10 reward to catch a sheep stealer. Descriptions were often florid. An itinerant horse dealer who defrauded Mr Wells with a forged £1 Bank of England note was 5ft. 8 inches high with a dark complexion and a thick upper lip, while his companion had a very full fresh face, was stout with a fair complexion and 5ft. 10 inches tall. Both were about 45 years old. They were pursued from Wisborough Green to Albury in Surrey by two members of the Society and found in bed with two women accomplices, who distracted the pursuers' attention long enough to permit the forgers to escape!

On another occasion Chas. Pullen was caught red-handed with a stolen goose egg in his hand. On being apprehended he offered his captor, Jas. Steen, a bribe of 1s. to say nothing, but he was refused. The Stenning family were persistent offenders and invariably came under suspicion when offences were reported and were then despatched to a magistrate 'with all convenient speed'. The Society engaged solicitors to press their case and virtually all the prosecutions were successful. At its peak in 1820 there were 47 members of the Wisborough Green Prosecuting Society, but when it was wound up in 1830 membership had fallen to 24.

Other Prosecuting Societies in West Sussex included those at Arundel, Chichester, Cowfold, Henfield, Horsham, Lancing, Lurgashall, Northchapel, Slinfold, Warnham and West Tarring. The areas covered varied widely from the parish at Warnham to the whole of the Rape of Chichester, one-third of West Sussex, for the Chichester Society. Most, like Wisborough Green, operated within a 10-15 miles radius. With the creation of proper police forces following Sir Robert Peel's legislation, the original role of these societies was removed. Many continued as social get-togethers with

80 *The stocks and whipping post in West Chiltington churchyard suggest the sorts of punishment meted out by parish vestries.*

SUSSEX.

PETWORTH HOUSE OF CORRECTION,
CALENDAR OF PRISONERS TRIED
At the General Quarter Sessions of the Peace held at PETWORTH,
On Monday, the 7th. Day of April, 1834.

15.	Bridger Lucas, alias William Bridger,	34	Geo. Farhill, Esq, 8th. Feb.	Stealing on the present day, at the parish of Appledram, seven pounds weight of horse hair, the property of Edward Dewey.	Transported for Seven Years.
16	William Worley,	34	G. B. Smith, Esq. 11th. March.	Stealing on the 8th. day of March instant, at the parish of Pulborough, one hat, value 6d. and a pair of quarter boots, value 5s. the property of Robert Tupper.	Discharged by Proclamation.
17	Charles Tuesley,	24	W. G. K. Gratwick, Esq. 14th. March.	Stealing on the first day of October last, at the parish of Tortington, two fowls, the property of John Gilbert.	Discharged by Proclamation.
18	Sarah Robinson,	58	Chris. Teesdale, Esq. 20th. March.	Feloniously maimed one sow pig, at the parish of Pagham, the property of William Payne.	6 Calendar Months to Hard Labour.
19	Henry Nye,	22	W. G. K. Gratwick, Esq. 27th. March.	Stealing on the 24th. January last, at the parish of Ferring, one drake and two ducks, the property of John Bennett.	Discharged by Proclamation.
20. 21	George Madgwick, Thomas Jinman,	20 23	R. B. Newland, Esq. 27th. March.	Stealing on the 27th. of March, 1833, at the parish of Midhurst, one duck, value 1s. the property of Thomas Arnold Davis, Esq.	20, Discharged by Proclamation. 21, Transported for Seven Years.
22	James Durrant,	17	Sir R. Jones, K. C. B. 9th. Jan.	Stealing on the 8th. day of January instant, at the parish of Kingstone, a pair of sea boots, the property of George Hay.	3 Calendar Months to Hard Labour.
33	Stephen Stammers,	28	Sir J. M. Lloyd, Bart. 4th. April	Stealing at the parish of Steyning, seven live hen fowls, 3 geese and one gander, value 4l. 14s. the property of	Transported for Seven Years.

81 *The Calendar of Prisoners tried at Petworth Quarter Sessions in 1834 and their sentences, including transportation.*

82 *Smugglers landing cargo near Shoreham.*

annual dinners at the *Three Crowns* (Wisborough Green), the *Onslow Arms* (Loxwood) or some other hostelry. Indeed, the Arundel Prosecuting Society still meets once a year at the *Norfolk Arms*, where the object is not to prosecute felons but to offer hospitality.

Smuggling

Smuggling has been a way of life along the Sussex coast for centuries and in the 18th and 19th centuries there were regular accounts of the seizure of contraband and its 'conveyance' to the customs houses at Chichester, Arundel and elsewhere. The smuggled cargoes were predominantly wine, spirits and tobacco and the quantities were substantial: 24 February 1783, 11,134 gallons of wine required four wagons to transport them to the customs house; 28 April 1783, over 90 casks of rum and brandy; 15 September 1788, 200 gallons of brandy and 105 gallons of wine; 21 March 1803, 393 tubs of geneva (gin) and 17 bags of tobacco. There were also specialised cargoes, such as black silk, used to trim mourning and funeral clothes, which was the preserve of a dressmaker in Lodsworth.

The smugglers employed a full range of tricks to avoid detection. They used flat-bottomed boats 'three deal planks wide' to transfer the cargoes from their 'luggers' in deep water through the shallower waters to the shore. They often floated the casks or left them hidden on shore for later collection by collaborators. At Wick they dropped them down a well until it was safe to reclaim them. The most ingenious scheme was discovered at Pagham where casks were funnelled into the harbour on the fast-flowing tide. In the most famous case, about 360 casks were collected from the banks near Sidlesham Mill after the tide had ebbed.

There was a constant battle of wits between the smugglers and the coastguards. The accounts in the newspapers invariably trumpet the successes of the coastguards but their 'clear-up rate' will never be known.

83 *Members of the infamous Hawkhurst Smuggling Gang beating Richard Hawkins, informer and thief, to death at the* Dog and Partridge *on Slindon Common.*

Frequently it was the riding-officers assisted by boat-officers who caught and apprehended the smugglers but occasionally, when prior 'intelligence' alerted them to an imminent operation, the coastguards invoked the help of the military. On 28 June 1830 the Bognor coastguards were supplemented by a party of the 15th Dragoons from Chichester Barracks and successfully intercepted a landing of contraband. The smugglers were sentenced to lengthy terms in 'Bridewell' (prison).

Capture was not always as efficient. Sometimes the smugglers were engaged at sea:

Last Thursday night [13 August 1789], as the crew of a smuggling cutter laden with spirits and tobacco were employed in running their cargo, they were surprised by the 'Stag Custom House cutter' belonging to Chichester, the officer of which despatched a boat, well manned and armed, to make the seizure of the smuggling boat; but the

84 *Coastguards on duty at East Preston, 1910.*

people coming, as they supposed, to their assistance, resolved in maintaining their cargo, which the crew of the 'Stag' perceiving, hove nearer shore and fired many shots over the smugglers, with a view to bringing them to a quiet surrender; but this not producing the desired effect, they then fired into the boat and killed Jesse Colman, dead on the spot, and desperately wounded two other smugglers ...

On 4 April 1835 James Whittington was shot in the leg while resisting capture west of Bognor coastguard station, had to have it amputated and died within hours of the operation, leaving a wife and three young children 'to lament his fate'. At the inquest the jury reached a verdict of 'justifiable homicide'. On another occasion, when smugglers were drowned, their dog 'must have suffered greatly as it swam to shore with two broken legs'. Sometimes they evaded capture. In 1770, smugglers 'being resolute and swearing' forced their way past the coastguards at Clymping and 'made off with seventeen horseloads of prohibited goods'.

Smugglers were not the only victims. In 1815 Lieutenant Cartwright, the Felpham coastguard, was 'unable to do duty for 12 days because of a skirmish'. Some years later two coastguards were found tied hand and foot in a ditch. The conflict was likened to 'a guerilla war between the smugglers and officers of the government' marked by 'organised resistance in which towns were besieged, battles fought, customs houses burnt down and the greatest atrocities committed'. The infamous murder of William Galley, a customs

house officer, and Daniel Chater, a shoemaker, in 1748 galvanised the 3rd Duke of Richmond to take personal responsibility for catching and convicting the 'fourteen notorious smugglers' and 'the execution of seven of the Bloody Criminals'. He vowed to eradicate the coast of this blight, but was attempting the impossible.

85   *Coastguard cottages at East Preston, 1910.*

86   *William Galley and David Chater were whipped so severely by the smugglers that they could not stay on the horse's back.*

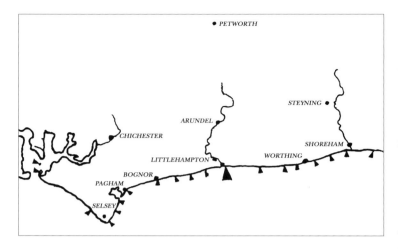

87 A map of the Coast Blockade stations between Chichester Harbour and Shoreham, 1825.

William Galley was given a Christian burial on 16 September 1749 at Rogate, where seven years later the curate and rector of Iping and Chithurst, John Denham, was murdered by Richard Aps, who stabbed him with a pitchfork in a furzefield where he was later discovered pinned to the ground.

The Coast Blockade: The Royal Navy's War on Smuggling 1817-31

The close of the Napoleonic Wars led to a renewed outbreak of smuggling, which threatened the fabric of society. In 1816 the government met this direct threat to its authority by transferring the fleet of revenue cutters from Customs to Admiralty control and placing the Preventive Water Guard under Treasury management. Neither of these measures succeeded. Loss of revenue was of secondary importance to stopping Kent and Sussex becoming ungovernable. The situation was so desperate that the government eagerly adopted a proposal to combat organised smuggling with a permanent beach cordon of armed naval troops called 'Sentinels'. It was expensive but preferable to anarchy and a loss of face, particularly with the French and American Revolutions of the late 18th century still fresh in people's minds. The question asked was 'Will Washington take America or the smugglers take England first'?

In 1817 the Coast Blockade was formed as a command within the Royal Navy, with a Commander-in-Chief reporting directly to the Admiralty, and is not to be confused with the Coast Guard, which was formed in 1822 under Customs control. Within five years the initial cordon of 80 personnel a few miles either side of Deal had grown to an unbroken blockade stretching 200 miles from Sheerness to Chichester Harbour and numbering over 3,000 Royal Navy officers and men to protect the vulnerable Kent and Sussex coastlines.

From 1816-25 the Commander-in-Chief was Captain William McCulloch, a tough taskmaster who revelled in the nickname 'Flogger Joey'. He administered discipline on a sliding scale of severity: disobedience 12 lashes, theft 18 lashes, drunkenness, neglect of duty and asleep at your post 24 lashes, and, reflecting his greatest problem of bribery and complicity, 36 lashes if absent without leave and found in a smuggler's house or company and 40 lashes for corruption.

Their brief was to prevent smuggling and 'attacks on the line'. They were a law enforcement force, 'an army of occupation', operating within the

88 *The Coast Blockade patrolling Shoreham Harbour in 1823.*

rules and traditions of the Royal Navy. They succeeded despite being outnumbered, inciting local hatred and facing an often hostile local magistracy such as John Wakefield of Worthing, who criticised Blockade witnesses and openly favoured the accused smugglers.

In Chichester a judge condemned a smuggler but the jury discharged him; the vicar of Sidlesham, the Rev. Goddard, was vociferous in his opposition, vigorously defending parishioners against accusations of smuggling; while in Selsey the fishermen objected to being harassed night and day by over zealous 'Sentinels'. Joe Robinson said their boats and houses were being targeted by search parties. They were expert in luring the Blockade away with false lights and flashes while landing the booty elsewhere. On their patrols the Blockade men kept warm by filling tarred canvas bags with straw, into which they put their feet, and packing them along the bottom of the boats.

In the 14 years of its existence the Blockade fought many battles: it is estimated 58 Blockade men and over 150 smugglers were killed. Gradually attitudes changed so that, whereas 82 smugglers were captured and only 49 convicted in 1825, in 1830 all 20 smugglers captured were convicted. When the Blockade was disbanded in 1831 the Coast Guard took over its role.

The Shipley Gang

After the Coast Blockade was set up smuggling gangs moved inland and diversified into highway robbery, house breaking, looting and pillaging, sheep stealing, poaching and similar illegal undertakings. They treated the law with contempt and terrorised entire districts.

Amongst the most notorious and audacious of these former smugglers was the Shipley Gang, whose territory embraced Horsham, Billingshurst, Nuthurst, Ashurst, Thakeham, Shermanbury and Rudgwick. Their base lay in Southwater Wood, near Shipley. They were cruel, cunning, ruthless, vicious and armed with pistols, although it is thought they stopped short of murder. They disguised themselves with masks and headgear.

There were numerous attempts to catch them but they were always a step ahead of their pursuers. On one occasion they were surrounded in a cottage, a constable knocking on the front door being a sign for reinforcements to enter through the back, but when the gang heard the knock they extinguished the lights and in the pitched battle which ensued they escaped.

Finally the parishes in the district decided to pool resources to rid themselves of the gang. The combined effort succeeded in capturing James 'Robin Hood' Rapley, Senior, the leader, and six of the gang, but the other six remained at large. Rapley was convicted and sentenced to death but he hung himself in his cell at Petworth Gaol before the sentence could be carried out. The death sentence for the other five was commuted to transportation to Australia.

James Longley assumed leadership of the remaining gang members but their freedom was short-lived and they were also transported to Australia. After serving 10 of his 14 years' sentence he was released and returned to Shipley to marry the woman he loved and had left behind, and who had waited for him to return as he had promised to do.

The 'Peacher' and the Press Gang

Smugglers exploited their connections to gain retribution against anyone who stepped out of line. At 8 o'clock on the evening of 27 February 1804 a gang of ten men dressed in round frocks and armed with clubs, a sword and pistol burst into a house on Cootham Common, Storrington, dragged William Souter out of bed, bound him and disappeared into the night. Mrs Souter and her young children cowered in the corner, witnessing the violent removal of their husband and father.

He had been seized by the Littlehampton Press Gang, who had the right to impress men for service in the Navy but not from as far afield as Storrington. They had been 'bribed' with money and brandy to remove Souter in revenge for his 'peaching' or informing on a gang of smugglers whose leader was his neighbour at the *Crown Inn*, Cootham Common. Souter had once been a 'rider' for the smugglers, bringing contraband inland from the coast to be distributed in the countryside, so he was conversant with the members and the organisation. Although he had gone straight for many years, 'peaching' on former colleagues was the worst violation of the code of conduct among thieves, often dealt with by death.

Despite his protestations and those of his wife and employer, Souter was taken under guard to Portsmouth where only the intervention of Thomas Broad, Comptroller of Customs for the port of Arundel,

VERY
SUPERIOR AND FAST TRAVELLING
BY SAFETY COACHES,
TO
LONDON,
Shoreham, Brighton, Lewes, Newhaven, Horsebridge, Eastbourne, Battle, Dover, Arundel, Littlehampton, Bognor, Chichester, Emsworth, Havant, and Portsmouth,
FROM J. SNOW'S SPREAD-EAGLE AND UNIVERSAL COACH OFFICE,
No. 20, SOUTH STREET, WORTHING.

TO LONDON,
THE SOVEREIGN and ACCOMMODATION, Safety Coaches, every Morning, at NINE o'Clock, to the Spread Eagle, Gracechurch Street, CITY, and Spread Eagle Office, 220, PICCADILLY, corner of the Regent Circus, and next door to Webb's Hotel ; from whence they return every Morning, at a Quarter before NINE.

Route—Through Horsham, Dorking, and Epsom.
Messrs. JOHN SNOW, HOWES, DAWSON, MITCHELL, HOLDEN, and W. CHAPLIN, Proprietors.
N. B. Parcels Booked to all parts of the Kingdom.

TO BRIGHTON,
PATENT SAFETY COACHES,
THE MAGNET, every Morning at Half-past NINE o'Clock, and returns from Brighton every Evening at FIVE.
THE ECLIPSE, every Evening at FIVE o'Clock, and returns from Brighton every Morning, at TEN.

The above Coaches go to the Spread Eagle Office, No. 18, Castle Square, Brighton, from whence the WONDER and HERO Coaches leave for HASTINGS every Morning (except Sundays) at NINE o'Clock.

TO PORTSMOUTH,
THE DEFIANCE, through Arundel, Chichester, and Havant, every day at Half-past TWELVE precisely, and returns from the George Hotel, Portsmouth, every Morning at NINE o'Clock.

Passengers and Parcels Booked for the above Coach at the Norfolk Arms, Arundel, and the Dolphin Hotel, Chichester.
J. SNOW & Co. Proprietors.

County Fire and Provident Life Office.

The London Daily and Weekly Newspapers to be had at the above Office, as stated on the other side.

to whom Souter had provided the information against the smugglers, obtained his release. On the morning of 15 March he walked the 19 miles from Havant to Arundel, arriving at Broad's house in a state of collapse as he had never recovered from the beating he received when he was captured. He was immediately put to bed and sent home by cart the next morning. Six days later he died.

His wife was destitute. Evidently the episode caused a stir in the neighbourhood sufficient for the Earl of Egremont to take up her case through his lawyer, William Tyler. Lieutenant Spry, commander of the Press Gang, and three members were tried and found guilty at the Sussex Lent Assizes in 1805. Spry claimed he was carrying out his duty and the others that they were merely acting on orders, but this defence did not wash.

The subsequent fortunes of the protagonists diverged markedly. James 'Old Gingerbread' Searle, landlord of the *Crown Inn*, died in 1806, Spry and Meeton, a member of the gang, served their sentences, and a reformed Meeton became a well-respected schoolmaster, while Robert Applegate, who

89 *A poster advertising a daily service from the south coast to London in 'Safety Stage Coaches'.*

had originally 'persuaded' Spry to impress Souter, lived to a ripe old age in Littlehampton on the proceeds of a fortune made as a wine and spirit merchant!

The Great East Grinstead Mail Robbery

At the beginning of the 19th century East Grinstead was a vital hub in the collection and distribution of mail. It served a wide area, including Croydon in Surrey, Crawley, Cuckfield and Lindfield. Mail from London and Brighton was unloaded and redirected to destinations throughout the district.

In those days mail coaches ran daily apart from Sunday. On Saturday night 19 July 1801 John Beaston (70) and his son William (27) lay in

90 Communication was maintained in the latter part of the 19th century by a daily delivery and collection of mail.

wait for the 7 p.m. mail coach from Brighton at Wall Hill just outside East Grinstead. As it approached they stepped into the road, stopped the coach, unhitched the horses, took them into an adjoining field and tied up the driver. They dragged the heavy, bulging mail bags into a nearby corn field and hid until the furore died down. They opened the letters and extracted Bank of England and country banknotes. When the bags were discovered a month or so later during harvest, the robbers had left over £9,350 behind. Their share was never discovered but they still had over £3,000 on them when they were finally caught later in the year in Liverpool, which suggests a lucrative haul.

John Beaston, a Scotsman, had settled in Edinburgh as an innkeeper after years in the merchant service. His wife died and he and his son became drifters, taking jobs wherever and whenever the opportunities arose. This peripatetic lifestyle finally brought them to Hartfield, Sussex, where they hatched and planned their audacious highway robbery. In an effort to set a false trail they moved to London, only returning to perpetrate the offence. They spent the night of 17 July at the *Rose and Crown* in Godstone and the night of 18 July at the *Blue Anchor* in Blindley Heath. These stays were their undoing as they were recognised and became suspects, and their descriptions were circulated and a 'hue and a cry' raised throughout England. They escaped detection by moving from place to place until they were finally

91 *Dick Turpin's cottage, East Grinstead, now the site of the police station.*

cornered when an ostentatious display of their new-found wealth created suspicion, and jealousy tempted an informer to claim the reward placed on their heads.

John and William Beaston were taken to Bow Street and thence to Horsham Gaol to await trial, which took place on 29 March 1802. Over thirty witnesses testified. The father admitted his guilt but attempted to deflect blame from his son, who denied complicity in the raid. It later emerged that William was not his son but a baby John had taken in at birth and treated as his own. William escaped from prison but was recaptured in a sewer. The jury, without absenting themselves, found both men guilty and passed a sentence of death.

On 17 April they were taken by cart from Horsham to Wall Hill attended by a Catholic priest and they 'behaved in a manner suitable to their wretched function'. They were 'launched into eternity' in front of over 3,000 spectators, on gallows especially erected in the field where they had committed the crime. This was customary at the time, hence the number of 'Gibbet's Fields'. Both men were buried in Horsham.

The Last Execution at Horsham
The ultimate punishment was meted out for a wide range of offences but it does not appear to have acted as a deterrent. The day of the Horsham Teg

92 Reputedly Dick Turpin making his get away by clearing a tollgate outside East Grinstead.

93 Public hangings were meant to be deterrents but they attracted large, curious crowds to witness the executions and participate in the ancillary activities.

Fair, 6 April 1844, dawned sunny and warm as people flocked from the surrounding villages into the small town. On this occasion their excursion had a sinister purpose, as an execution was scheduled at noon.

Curiosity drew over 3,000 to witness the event. They gathered early to take up prime positions in the Carfax and adjacent streets. The bar owners expressed the wish that an execution would take place every day. Drunkards were soon confessing that they were worse criminals than the victim about to be executed. Costermongers from Brighton sold oranges to quench thirst and claimed 'they would melt in the mouth like butter, sugar outside, brandy inside and rind that will make good boot soles'. Peddlers jostled their way between the crowds selling printed sheets containing a crude ballad which they claimed was 'The Last Confession' of the accused man.

At noon a posse of police brought in for the occasion took up positions in front of the gallows to prevent the crowd from getting too close. Inside the gaol a procession formed. At its head were the chaplain and under sheriff and their attendants; next came the condemned man supported by a turnkey, followed by the executioner and court officials. All were bareheaded and wound their way through the labyrinth of corridors in the gaol, halting at the foot of the stairs to the room which led to the gallows.

A composed prisoner held his hat in his hand and ascended the stairs after the chaplain and hangman, walking purposefully onto the platform between two lines of officials and attendants. The babble of the crowd ceased immediately. While the condemned man was being pinioned the chaplain said final prayers. The executioner went below and drew the bolt. As the trap fell a young boy crouching on a low wall sobbed bitterly. He was John Lawrence's brother.

In early March Lawrence and a compatriot had stolen a carpet from Collins, house furnishers in Brighton. They were chased, caught and taken to Brighton Police Station where they were interrogated by Police Inspector Henry Soloman in the presence of the two constables who had apprehended them. After questioning, during which he was evasive, Lawrence became increasingly agitated. Periods of questioning were punctuated with lengthy silences. During one such interval Soloman turned his back to tend the fire which gave Lawrence an opportunity to grab the poker and deliver a fatal blow to Soloman's head. He was carried from the room unconscious and died a few hours later.

The culprit was a young, good looking, married man of about 25 years of age who declined to give his name for fear of disgracing his family. When he appeared before the magistrates he was recognised as John Lawrence from a respectable Tunbridge Wells family. His father had died and his mother's re-marriage marked his downward spiral into a life of crime. He drank heavily and fell in with a gang of robbers led by the notorious 'Hastings Bet'. He fell out with her following a quarrel and moved to Brighton.

He was sentenced to death for murdering Inspector Soloman and held in the House of Correction,

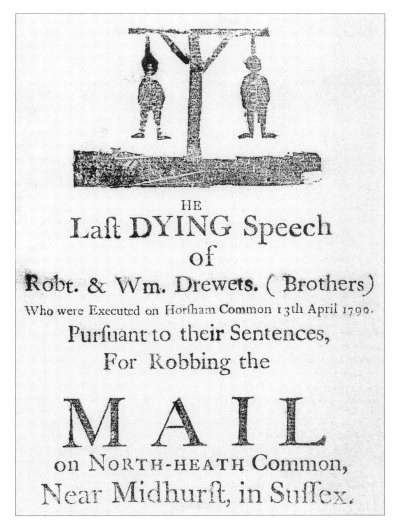

HE
Laſt DYING Speech
of
Robt. & Wm. Drewets. (Brothers)
Who were Executed on Horſham Common 13th April 1799.
Purſuant to their Sentences,
For Robbing the
MAIL
on NORTH-HEATH Common,
Near Midhurſt, in Suſſex.

94 *The alleged confession of the Drewett Brothers, highwaymen, executed on Horsham Common in 1799 for robbing the mail at North Heath Common, near Midhurst, as sold by peddlers at their execution.*

95 *Pen portraits of two Sussex lawyers at Horsham Assizes, 1815.*

Lewes. His only visitors were his uncle and younger brother. The hangman cried uncontrollably as he pinioned Lawrence, who, in his final weeks, had repented, prayed and sang hymns. He died with the words 'Lord, be merciful to me a sinner' on his lips.

Haigh and the Acid Bath Murders

John George Haigh lived in Room 404 in the fashionable *Onslow Court Hotel*, Kensington. He was 39 years of age, about 5ft. 8 inches tall, elegant, with a clipped moustache, looking for all the world like the successful city gent. His immaculate appearance and expensive suits, highly polished shoes, dark brylcreemed hair, sophisticated suave manner, wide range of interests, and accomplished conversation meant he was good company and readily accepted amongst the 'retired gentlefolk' who inhabited the hotel. His taste in expensive, luxury sports cars and his propensity for taking guests for 'spins' endeared him to them. He had a reputation for 'fine living' and 'money was no object'. He enjoyed this lifestyle for more than four years but it was soon to be brought to an abrupt halt.

96 *The wax figure of John George Haigh, the acid bath murderer in Madame Tussaud's.*

On the afternoon of 19 February 1949 he volunteered to drive one of his acquaintances at the hotel, 69-year-old Constance Lane, to the police

97 *Haigh's unkempt lair in Giles Yard, Leopold Road, Crawley with some of his equipment.*

station to make enquiries about the disappearance of her best friend, Mrs Olive Durand-Deacon, a wealthy widow in her seventies, who had not returned from a shopping trip to the Army & Navy store. He accompanied her into the station and entered into conversation with the duty officer, WPS Lambourne. Afterwards he drove her back, reassuring her that there was an innocent explanation.

In fact, Haigh had arranged to collect Mrs Durand-Deacon from the Army & Navy store and take her for a trip to his factory in Crawley to show her how their joint venture to manufacture 'artificial nails' (an idea in advance of its time) was proceeding. She showed no surprise when Haigh pulled up at Giles Yard, Leopold Road, a rather remote, decrepit, run-down site comprising a shabby brick building, into which she was ushered, and a yard full of rusting tin drums, redundant car engines and other paraphernalia. She had barely got inside when Haigh drew his .38 Enfield revolver and shot

98 *A police display of Haigh's 'tools of his trade', including his weapon and the oil drums in which he stuffed his victims.*

99 *A reconstruction of Haigh wearing protective clothing and a mask.*

her in the back of the head. She died instantly.

Haigh then went through a ritual in which he slit her neck with a pen-knife and allowed the blood to drip into a glass before drinking it. Mrs Durand-Deacon was a large, 14-stone woman, immaculately coiffured, wearing an expensive fur coat and dripping with jewellery. He removed all the valuables before trussing her up like an oven ready turkey and dragging her over the filthy floor, forcing her, with some difficulty, into an oil drum lying on its side. Haigh then righted the drum, pumped in sulphuric acid, fastened the lid and walked confidently to his waiting Alvis to drive back to Kensington.

Giles Yard was an outbuilding belonging to Hurstlea Products, a small engineering and tool-making concern owned by Edward Jones, who had come into contact with Haigh through the business. They became friends because Haigh used his contacts to obtain custom for Jones who, in return, gave him free run of this derelict workshop as a 'research lab' to conduct 'experiments' in acid conversion, some of which benefited the firm, while others clearly did not! Haigh boasted to his associates that he was the director of this company and that it was his main source of income, thus deflecting any suspicions about his lavish lifestyle, which was in reality funded by an old colleague, McSwann, who had made a fortune running amusement arcades and whom Haigh met just after the end of the Second World War in his favourite watering hole, *The Goat*. Haigh killed McSwann and his parents in London and took them to Crawley to dispose of their bodies.

When this money ran out he befriended Dr and Mrs Rosalie Henderson, whom he met when viewing their house at 22 Ladbroke Grove with the intention of purchasing it. They spent a weekend together at the *Metropole* in Brighton, from where Haigh took Arthur Henderson to the Giles Yard premises with predictable consequences. Rosalie was distraught when her husband failed to return so Haigh took her to Crawley on the pretext that her husband was ill and had been taken to hospital. She suffered the same fate and was stuffed into the same drum on top of her decaying husband. By now the newspapers had got hold of the serial killings and the method of disposal of the victims and their front pages led with lurid headlines such as 'Hunt for the Vampire'.

Haigh had ensured in the McSwann and Henderson cases that they made over their money and property to him. In the case of the former this amounted to over £6,000 and in the latter £7,771. By the time he killed Olive Durand-Deacon he was in debt through gambling and creditors were about to close in to secure what he owed. In accordance with his pattern, he sold her valuables to pawnbrokers, but their sale only realised £119.

WPS Lambourne had shared her intuitive suspicions with other officers and they checked Haigh out. She discovered that he had convictions on 12 charges in 1934 and 1937 for fraud and obtaining money by false pretences in Leeds and Surrey, and for theft in London in 1941 for which he received 21 months' hard labour in Lincoln Gaol. The police in Horsham and Crawley were alerted, searched the Giles Yard premises and found incriminating evidence, including documents and clothes linking Haigh to the Hendersons and Mrs Durand-Deacon, but no bodies.

The game was up. Haigh was convicted of the murders of the McSwanns, Hendersons and Olive Durand-Deacon and he claimed he had killed three more victims and gone through the same routine. He made a signed confession, and at 8.45 a.m. on Wednesday 10 August 1949 Britain's most notorious serial murderer since Jack the Ripper was hanged in Wandsworth Prison by Albert Pierrepoint, whose principal occupation was landlord of the *Help the Poor Struggler* public house.

Neither before nor since has anyone disposed of their victims by drowning them in sulphuric acid. The murders were premeditated and Haigh showed no remorse; in the condemned cell he wrote an 'exclusive' for the *News of the World* to be published after his death. Perhaps the most fortunate person was his 20-year-old Crawley girlfriend, who never suspected him and whom he took to the cinema to see *Dark Passage* and *Great Expectations* on the nights he committed the murders. Haigh moved from a seedy one-bedroom flat in Queen Anne's Gate to the life of luxury which he sustained, undetected, for six years.

Five

WAR AND PEACE

Being on the south coast, West Sussex has been in the forefront of a succession of threats, invasions and wars, each of which has left its mark. The Romans bequeathed a sumptuous palace at Fishbourne and impressive villas, such as that at Bignor, and an infrastructure of roads, such as Stane Street, as a legacy of their military strategy and might. The Normans defended their gains with a network of castles and laid the foundations of boroughs in order to consolidate their hold on the country. During the medieval period King and Country had to repel numerous invaders, but the event which has most caught the imagination is the engagement with the Spanish fleet in the reign of Elizabeth I.

The Spanish Armada

> As Philip IV of Spain prepared his Invincible Armada, Elizabeth I acting on the wise counsels of Raleigh, Drake, Frobisher and Hawkins promptly strengthened her defences and put the most vulnerable parts of her kingdom into such a condition as to defy invasion. The high-sheriffs of the most assailable counties received the royal command to examine and strengthen their respective sea-boards.

'A Survey of the Coast of Sussex 1587 with a view to its defence against Foreign Invasion, and especially the Spanish Armada' described the action taken:

> At the coast unto Pagham Beacons, for the moste part goode landings, and therefore not sufficiently garded, but have made Trenches and flankers (side or lateral earthworks). At littel Hampton haven the entire to Arundel to be also fortified for the planting of ii demi-culverings and ii sacres [cannon, here referred to by terms used in falconry] for the faster garding thereof and no need of entrenchinge but at speciall places where Stades or Beacons are ...

'Stade' is a local term signifying a place on the shore where vessels may be run aground for pleasure, discharging of cargoes or naval attack. Beacons were piles of brushwood or furze erected on elevated positions, which, when set fire to, would communicate news of an impending invasion far and wide. These piles were under the superintendence of a person who rode a light horse or 'hobby' and thence received the name of 'hobilier'. His duty was

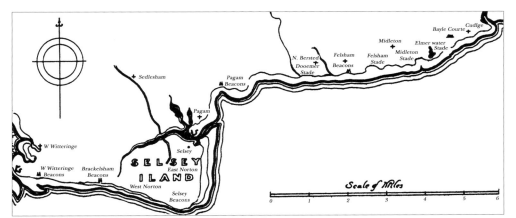

100 *A map of the Spanish Armada defences along the West Sussex coast showing the beacons.*

to ride from beacon to beacon, and to direct their being lighted if the fleet approached the coast during daylight. (The nation's security depended on the hobilier riding faster than ships sailed.)

> At Shoreham also necessary to be fortified for the planting of i dimy-culvering and ii sacres and between littel Hampton and Shoreham goode landings for the most part are reasonably well garded with water between the Beach and firme lande save only next the mille and that muddy with sedges …

Additional 'Topographical Notes' attached to the Survey give a measure of the distance the coastline has receded in the last 400 years. Sidlesham Tide Mill was accessible to 'barks' of 40 tons until about 1870, when Pagham Harbour was reclaimed for agriculture. It spelt the end of the mill despite the harbour being inundated after a storm in 1910 which breached the retaining shingle bank.

It is interesting to observe the landmarks selected for display. 'Cissbury and Chanctonbury are two well known heights of the South Downs and each crowned with a Celtic entrenchment', a reference to the Iron-Age hill forts which cap their summits(Lower, M.A., *A Survey of the Coast of Sussex 1587*, 1870, pp.3-6). The Spanish Armada did not worry the Sussex shore but the system of beacons and gun emplacements continued to provide

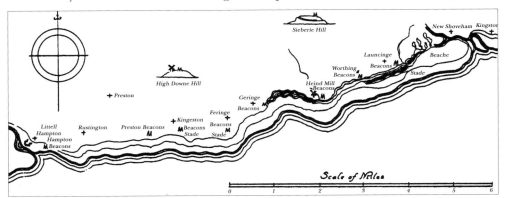

101 Spanish Armada defences along the West Sussex coast.

protection for many years. It is no coincidence that the monarch's coronation and jubilee celebrations are still marked by lighting beacons, but few are aware of their origin.

The Un-Civil and 'Unnaturrall Warre': The Siege of Chichester, 1642

Battles were fought not only against foreign foes but also internally, between opposing forces. The West Sussex gentry were staunchly Royalist at the time of the civil war while the citizens of the towns and cities were mainly Protestant and rebellious against increases in taxation and the free billeting of Royalist soldiers. In Chichester the hostility was accentuated by the Cathedral Close's (the south-west quarter of the city) being exempt from town dues and the clergy reintroducing papist practices.

The town was a key prize for the Parliamentarians because it stood in the way of Royalist advances from the west and it controlled an important stretch of the coastline. Chichester was in an unusual position because both parties had a significant presence there, and while the light horses of the Royalist cavalry drilled daily in the Cathedral Close the Parliamentarians paraded in the north-east quarter. In August 1642 the citizens of Chichester resolved

> to adventure their lives and fortunes for the defence of the true Protestant religion, the Lawes of the Lord, the Privileges and Liberty of the Subject, and against anyone who oppose them.

They backed their words with action. They strengthened the fortifications by borrowing seven cannon and ten barrels of gunpowder from Portsmouth Castle. This was a direct challenge to the Royalists and the stand-off could not continue indefinitely. The Royalists, reinforced by Sir Edward Ford of Uppark with 100 horsemen and a Trained Band he had recruited from the county *en route*, captured the cannon partly by force and partly by trickery. The Royalist triumph was complete on 16 November 1642 when the Mayor read the Royal Pardon at the Market Cross, prohibiting the Parliamentary Ordinance from raising money for an army.

In December Parliament sent Sir William Waller, M.P. for Andover, with 6,000 men and six cannon with a range of 2,000 yards and capable of direct hits at 500 yards, to recapture Chichester. The army camped on the 'Broils' (Broyle) north of the city where higher ground provided a panorama over the city. Waller mounted his battery and bombarded the walls. He moved 'within halfe a musket shot' of the North Gate where the cannon shot through the gateway into the market place. Reinforcements arrived from a successful battle at Arundel to command the South Gate.

In desperation the Royalists set fire to the suburb of St Pancras outside the East Gate and to St Bartholomew's outside the West Gate so as to provide a smokescreen, but to no avail. Waller kept up the bombardment for seven days and forced the garrison to seek terms of surrender. Those offered

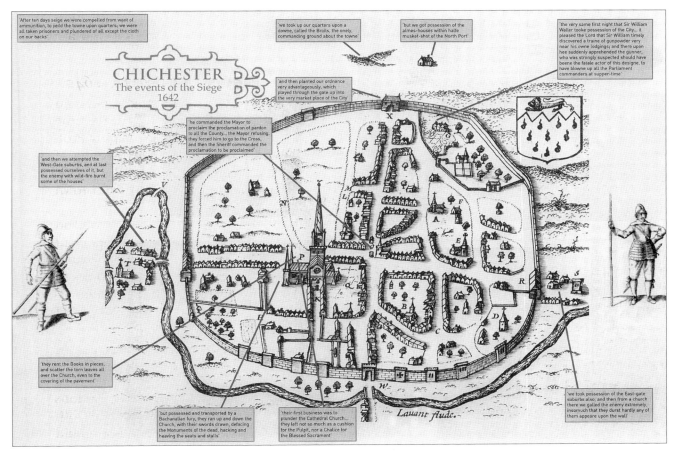

'After ten days seige we were compelled from want of ammunition, to yeild the towne upon quarters; we were all taken prisoners and plundered of all except the cloth on our backs'

'we took up our quarters upon a downe, called the Broils, the onely commanding ground about the towne'

'but we got possession of the almes-houses within halfe musket-shot of the North Port'

'the very same first night that Sir William Waller tooke possession of the City... it pleased the Lord that Sir William timely discovered a traine of gunpowder very near his owne lodgings; and there upon hee suddenly apprehended the gunner, who was strongly suspected should have beene the fatale actor of this designe, to have blowne up all the Parliament commanders at supper-time'

CHICHESTER
The events of the Siege
1642

'and then planted our ordnance very advantageously, which played through the gate up into the very market place of the City'

'he commanded the Mayor to proclaim the proclamation of pardon to all the County... the Mayor refusing, they forced him to go to the Cross, and then the Sheriff commanded the proclamation to be proclaimed'

'and then we attempted the West-Gate suburbs, and at last possessed ourselves of it, but the enemy with wild-fire burnt some of the houses'

'they rent the Books in pieces, and scatter the torn leaves all over the Church, even to the covering of the pavement'

'but possessed and transported by a Bachanalian fury, they ran up and down the Church, with their swords drawn, defacing the Monuments of the dead, hacking and heaving the seats and stalls'

'their first business was to plunder the Cathedral Church... they left not so much as a cushion for the Pulpit, nor a Chalice for the Blessed Sacrament'

'we took possession of the East-gate suburbs also; and then from a church there we galled the enemy extremely, insomuch that they durst hardly any of them appeare upon the wall'

Lauant flude.

were unacceptable and it vowed to fight on, but it was outnumbered and the artillery was no match for that of the Parliamentarians. On 29 December Waller entered the city victorious and despatched the most important Royalists, 'men that cannot doe but mischiefe and only fit for a plantacion', including Sir Edward Ford, to London as prisoners. The common soldiers were released.

The Parliamentarian soldiers, led and encouraged by Waller and his officers, went on the rampage, ransacking and looting the cathedral. Bruno Ryves, later Dean of Chichester, has left a 'vivid description' of the plunder. On 30 December the looters,

> went unto the Vestery, there they seize the Vestments and Ornaments of the Church, together with the Consecrated Plate ... they left not so much as a cushion for the Pulpit, nor a Chalice for the Blessed Sacrament; the Commanders having in person executed the covetous part of Sacrilege, they leave the destructive and spoyling part to be finished by the Common Soldiers; brake down the Organs and dashing the pipes with their pole-axes. They break the Rail around the Communion Table which was done with such fury that the Table itself did not escape their madness and was broken in pieces by them ... they force open all the locks wherein the singing men

102 *A map, adapting John Speed's 1610 plan, illustrating the tactics and progress of the Siege of Chichester.*

laid up their Common Prayer-Books, Gowns and Surplesses; they rent the books in pieces and scatter the torn leaves all over the Church and Pavement ... these Monuments [of the Kings of England] they deface and mangle with their hands and swords, as high as they could reach and to show their Love and Zeal for the Protestant Religion one of these miscreants picked out the eyes of King Edward the sixth's picture ...

[On the following Tuesday they had a Thanksgiving Service in the cathedral after which] they ran up and down the Church, with their swords drawn, defacing the Monuments of the dead, hacking and hewing the Seats and Stalls, scratching and scraping the painted Walls; Sir William Waller and the rest of the Commanders standing by as spectators, and approvers of these Barbaric Impieties.

Having made what spoyl they could in the Cathedral, they rush out thence and break upon a Parish Church, standing on the Northside of the Cathedral, called the Sub-Deanery; there they tear the Common Prayer-Books; and because many things in the Holy Bible make strongly against them, they marked it in divers places with a black cole; they stole the Ministers Surpless and Hood and all the linnen for Communion; and finding no more Plate but the Chalice, they stole that too, which they brake in pieces, to make a just and equal dividend amongst themselves.

Sir Arthur Haslerigg, having Intelligence by a treacherous officer of the Church where the remainder of the Plate was, commanded his servants to break down the Wainscot around the room, which was quickly done, they having brought Crows of Iron for that purpose along with them ... Sir Arthur, dancing and skipping cryed out, 'there Boys, there Boys, heark, heark, it Rattles, it Rattles'.

Such behaviour was hardly in keeping with the professed objects of the Siege, and the revenge the soldiers inflicted was hardly commensurate with the perceived excesses of worship. It is suggested the soldiers considered the spoils of victory compensation for the month's pay owing them.

The only other battle of note fought in Sussex during the Civil War was the Siege of Arundel, 13 December 1643-6 January 1644, at which Waller was again victor, starving the Royalist garrison into submission. The other confrontations were little more than skirmishes.

Second World War

During the Second World War pill boxes (named after the boxes containing Queen Victoria's medicinal tablets) dotted the coastline, dragon's teeth and rolls of barbed wire were strung out along beaches and other accessible landing places to deter the enemy and public access. Some were thatched and others camouflaged as beach huts, ice cream kiosks, newsagents and tea rooms. A few still survive.

Most prominent amongst the many aerodromes and auxiliary airfields, such as those at Apuldram, Merston and Westhampnett, and decoy airfields, such as that at East Wittering, was RAF Tangmere. It ranked alongside Biggin Hill and Scampton for its exploits during the Battle of Britain, D-Day and other battles, and was associated with flying 'aces' such as Douglas Bader, Neville Duke and Johnny Johnson.

Bayley's Farm was commandeered for use and continued as an airfield until 1970. It suffered its worst losses on 16 August 1940 when considerable damage was inflicted by enemy bombing. During the raid 13 personnel were killed and 20 seriously injured, three Blenheims, and seven Hurricanes were destroyed on the ground, hangars were burnt out and others incapacitated. Many were buried in the cemetery attached to Tangmere parish church alongside crew who crashed along the coastal strip at places such as Worthing, where a Spitfire plunged 2,000 feet out of control, Bosham and West Dean, as well as airmen, both British and German, washed up on nearby Channel beaches. Missions to repatriate French agents were also vulnerable and many are buried in Brookwood, Woking.

103 *Lieutenant Commander Robert Lochner experimenting with a Li-Lo in his garden pond at Rats Castle, Linchmere, where he developed the 'bombardon'. He also invented 'degaussing', which negated Hitler's secret weapon, the non-contact magnetic mine, by effectively making the ships invisible to the mines.*

While the contribution of aerodromes such as Tangmere and Ford is well known, the roles of the auxiliary forces have figured less prominently and justify devoting space to the less publicised aspects of the Second World War.

Li-Lo

In May 1942 Winston Churchill wrote the following minute to Lord Louis Mountbatten, Chief of Combined Operations:

> They must float up and down with the tide. The anchor problem must be mastered … Let me have the best solution worked out. Don't argue the matter. The difficulties will argue for themselves.

For the first time in history an invading army was being instructed to take its own harbour to an enemy-held shore. The Operation Overlord planners had to supply the forces with daily supplies weighing 20 lb. (30 lb. for American soldiers!). Every division needed 600 tons daily and five divisions were earmarked to land on D-Day with others following. The strategists could not rely on securing an enemy port or dropping supplies; they had to take it with them by sea.

Churchill's answer was to construct artificial harbours. The specification required a breakwater to isolate the landing zone from the English Channel, a quay for ships to unload and jetties to take the goods onshore. Prefabricated sections had to be capable of being towed across the 100-mile wide Channel commencing on D-Day +1 and be fully operational within a fortnight. The harbour had to have a minimum lifespan of 90 days.

The responsibility for solving this problem and designing the solution fell on the shoulders of Lieutenant Commander Robert Lochner, a young

Imperial War Museum, H38674

104 *Completed concrete caissons (Phoenixes), part of the 'mulberry' (prefabricated) harbour, parked off Selsey ready to be towed across the Channel to Normandy after D-Day.*

RNVR scientist from Hammer in the parish of Linchmere. The idea for a floating sea wall evolved from experiments he conducted at Rats Castle, Hammer. He noticed in the bath that his bag-type flannel calmed the ripples in the water. He developed the idea in the trout pond in the garden. His wife sewed a metal keel on the family Li-Lo, which he floated on the pond while she simulated wave action by paddling a cricket bat. It proved his theory that the force of waves could be suppressed by a floating barrier.

More sophisticated experiments on top secret 'Li-Lo' followed under strict security. The solution was a series of gigantic rubber airbags with keels made of hollow tubes of reinforced concrete capable of carrying 12,000 tons of stores and 2,500 vehicles daily. They were protected by hollow steel caissons shaped like a Maltese Cross. Lochner was summoned to accompany Churchill to Quebec for a top level Operation Overlord conference and subsequently to Washington to give President Roosevelt and Winston Churchill a 20-minute presentation on the capability of his idea.

To deceive the Germans, aerial photography covered a far more extensive area than the Normandy beaches. Supplementary information was obtained by members of the Special Boat Squadron operating from bases in and around Bognor Regis, who sent over small parties of experts to take depth soundings, soil samples, tidal measurements and other data. The success of part of the operation was due in no small measure to the inventive genius of Robert Lochner who received £1,000 in recognition of his exceptional contribution.

Mulberry Harbours

Selsey suffered 31 air raids during the Second World War. It was a 'no-go' area and residents had to show special passes. The socialite Lady Diana

Cooper had a holiday home, West House, at the sea end of Barrack Lane, Aldwick and she recalled, just before D-Day,

> the sea verge ... like a redoubtable barbican, now an area barred to non-residents. Most surprising there were mulberries floating some distance from my garden wall. The locals noticed them no longer and would say they were some form of submarine defence. The English were, by then, used to cover stories, and accepted ignorance with relief.

The mysterious giant floating blocks studded across Aldwick Bay were the best-kept secret of the war. Bognor inhabitants boasted of a new amphibious housing estate being built off-shore; in Bosham they told tales of the new concrete bridge across the Channel; but in Selsey they knew that the skyscrapers jutting out of the sea were the surprise element in the D-Day landings, because they were being assembled there.

Over one million tons of concrete, 50,000 tons of steelwork, six miles of piers and 120 miles of steel cables had to be in place to receive the mulberry sections, which were then connected like a giant 'meccano' set to form two 'landing bridges'.

A day after the initial D-Day landings a fleet of over 140 tugs pulled out of Aldwick Bay towing floating rafts carrying various mulberry structures. In less than a week the artificial harbours had been disembarked and the pontoons carried 74,000 troops, 10,000 vehicles and 17,000 tons of weapons, fuel and food, making a massive contribution to the war effort. A surviving relic of a mulberry pontoon remains to this day off Pagham Harbour as a potent reminder of the Bay's role in 'The Longest Day'.

Dads Army or Murder Bands

At 9 p.m. on Tuesday 14 May 1940 Anthony Eden broadcast to the nation:

> I want to speak to you tonight about the form of warfare the Germans have been employing so extensively against Holland and Belgium – namely, the dropping of troops by parachute behind the main defensive lines. Since the war began the Government has received countless enquiries from all over the Kingdom from men of all ages, who for one reason or another, are not at present engaged on military service, and who wish to do something for the defence of their country. Well, here is your opportunity. We want large numbers of men, who are British subjects between the ages of 17 and 65, to come forward and offer their services. The name of the new force which is to be raised will be the 'Local Defence Volunteers' – this title describes the duties in three words.

He proceeded to define the role of the LDV, variously parodied by the comedians of the day as the 'Last Ditch Venture' or 'Look, Duck and Vanish', in greater detail. When on duty the volunteers would be members of the Armed Forces but continue to live at home. They would carry out their normal day jobs and would not be paid, but they would receive a uniform and arms. The length of service was the duration of the war. Volunteers were invited to register at the nearest police station.

105 *The first 'Home Guard' volunteer signs on.*

No sooner had Eden finished speaking than police stations all over the country were swamped by men wanting to 'sign on'. Within 24 hours 250,000 had answered the appeal and by the end of June nearly 1,500,000 were 'on the books'. There are numerous anecdotes about the age limits being 'elastic', with under-17-year-olds convincing recruiting officers of their 'maturity' and over-65s of their 'youth'. Les Garrett manned the coastal battery at Aldwick, the only one between Selsey Bill and Littlehampton, which consisted of two First World War naval guns, and he was 15 years of age.

Although lampooned retrospectively in the TV comedy series 'Dads Army', the Home Guard, renamed on 23 July 1940, performed an invaluable service to the country. They were the local 'eyes and ears', protecting key targets and installations, patrolling the coastline, monitoring suspected 'fifth columnists', apprehending anyone acting suspiciously, including a birdwatcher at Pagham Harbour, defending shot-down enemy planes, examining ID cards and a diverse range of other duties. They were highly visible, using any excuse for a parade. Weapons were in short supply so they drew lots or improvised, even throwing beach pebbles at low flying Focke Wolfs.

The Home Guard was stood down in December 1945. The 70,000 West Sussex force disbanded in a series of 'farewell parades'. The overall cost in the county was estimated at £1 million but per Home Guardsman that worked out at only 5s., value for money. Only five died on duty from 1,206 nation-wide. The Germans announced they would treat them as 'murder bands' or terrorists, but they didn't have the opportunity to carry out their threat.

Operation Pied Piper

Britain was poorly prepared for the outbreak of war in 1939. The impact of aerial warfare in the Spanish Civil War created panic in the Ministry of Health and the Board of Education, who were responsible for mass evacuations from the large urban areas. It impressed upon them the urgency of preparing a plan of action.

West Sussex was one of the most important reception areas for evacuees, mostly from London. It had a target of 100,000 but the 'official' numbers did not turn up, although they were compensated by the 'private' evacuees who 'infiltrated West Sussex from a variety of administrative areas' and eventually

comprised 26 per cent of the total. The 'drift back' from West Sussex due to homesickness was not as pronounced as in other reception areas.

The efficiency of the reception areas did not match the despatching areas, although in Horsham 510 evacuees from Streatham were processed and dispersed to their billets in 45 minutes. In Singleton, however, 40 households were scheduled to receive evacuees but only four materialised, causing consternation. The rates of 10s. 6d. per week for one evacuee and 8s. 6d. each if there were two or more were inferior to the rates paid by those who made 'private' arrangements. As a result a huge range of accommodation was utilised, including holiday camps, old railway carriages and village halls.

Pressure on schools was so severe that many had to operate double-shifts and a few treble-shifts. Additional space was found in Petworth House, Bishop's Palace, Chichester, Stoughton Manor library, the *Walnut Tree* pub, Runcton, and scouts, church and village halls. As the South Coast became the front line, competition from the Army for lodging increased. In Poling the Army took over the school, which had to move into the vicarage and two council cottages.

On 29 August 1942 the head, an assistant and 24 children were killed when an enemy bomb flattened Petworth Junior School. In Selsey, despite

107 *A crashed German plane (Hermann) on Pagham Beach, 19 September 1940.*

protests, the Army installed a searchlight and anti-aircraft guns in the playground of a school occupied by physically handicapped children making it a legitimate military target. It was attacked by a German fighter which dived straight down the searchlight beam, killing the headmaster, school secretary and a pupil. The next day the school was moved to Cheshire! The school in Pagham was surrounded with barbed wire.

There is little wonder that the predominant cause of absence from school at this time was 'lack of sleep', and with frequent diving for cover or shelter it is no surprise that 'Barbara Holden is being kept away from school by her mother who will not let her sit again in a damp ditch'.

Evacuees became fully involved in the war effort in a huge range of activities, from digging trenches to knitting clothes, running messages to collecting salvage, helping farmers, picking blackberries and investing in national savings. Teachers were equally involved, in the Home Guard, as air-raid wardens, and in other capacities. There is some evidence that children were exploited as cheap labour and the head at Broadwater gave parents and guardians the ultimatum, 'school or potato harvest'. Holidays were certainly curtailed or non-existent as children were kept busy.

Generally there were few cases of anti-social behaviour, but some of the South Londoners were 'real terrors'. In Worthing an outbreak of pilfering was attributed to a Normal Public Assistance Committed School but was soon brought under control. In Broadwater the headteacher of a Jewish Orphanage School, 'an unbelievably stupid man', refused to accept 'gentiles'. But, considering one junior school in Worthing had to assimilate 336 children from 127 different schools, and a small rural school took 35 children from 13 London schools, and it took eight weeks to reassemble Henry Thornton School from Clapham after its pupils had been dispersed far and wide, it is to the Education Authority's credit that it coped so well. WSCC purchased two second-hand coaches and '100 bicycles' for the 'conveyance of senior children from country districts to secondary schools in urban areas'. Cycles and protective clothing were given to 60 pupils billeted in villages around Storrington to enable them to attend the secondary school. In retrospect, the ability to absorb so many evacuees in such a short time and maintain a semblance of normality was 'truly astounding'.

108 *Graves of young British and German airmen in the cemetery at Tangmere parish church.*

Camp Schools

In 1939 a National Camp Corporation Ltd was set up with £1,200,000 of government money to build the first 50 of a projected 100 Camp Schools throughout the country, each to house around 300 children. By autumn 1940, 30 had been opened. The first two to be completed were near Horsham. They were partly a response to the need to evacuate schools from vulnerable urban locations, partly an attempt to give urban children the

109 *A bomb crater and its aftermath at Frampton's Nursery, Angmering, 1940.*

110 *Children being shepherded by the Home Guard away from barbed wire which prevented access to Worthing beach during the Second World War.*

experience of boarding in a healthy environment, and partly broadening the curriculum with a wide range of extra-mural activities.

Wedges Farm, Horsham was taken over by Wilson's Grammar School, Camberwell, an aided London County Council school, in 1940. Cooper's Farm, also near Horsham, was occupied by Tor Hove School from Leyton Local Educational Authority. The former was a single sex school admitting pupils from good social backgrounds and providing a high standard of education, while the latter was a mixed school from a deprived area with low academic standards.

111 *Evacuees from Oliver Goldsmith School, London arriving at Billingshurst station in 1941.*

The numbers at Tor Hove Camp School fell and West Sussex County Council augmented the numbers with their own 'difficult' pupils. An Inspector's Report in 1943 labelled it 'a troublesome camp' which gave 'an impression of moribundity'. This was attributed to a combination of the social mix, a loss of identity in moving and an LEA which did not subscribe to the boarding school ethos. Conversely, Wilson's School was very successful.

112   Camp School, Wedges Farm, near Horsham.

113   *Weighing and measuring pupils at Wedges Farm Camp School.*

The 'experiment' had powerful supporters and Ernest Bevin was eager for it to continue post-war so that a residential element could be introduced into state schools. He advocated extending it by converting old POW camps. Prohibitive costs and impracticability prevented its continuing but the principle has been accepted by most LEAs and residential experience is now provided in one form or another.

The clinching blow to the continuation of Camp Schools was the findings of a study comparing the physical measurements and well-being of individual pupils in 1940 and 1944. The results were 'bewildering' and 'somewhat disconcerting' because they concluded that living and studying in the open air had not conferred the anticipated benefits. The author commented:

> … the inference of the study would appear to be that it is better for a child to stay in East London, sleeping irregular hours in ill-ventilated shelters eating fish and chips than to have fresh air conditions in one of our Camp Schools with regular hours of sleep and plenty of fresh, well prepared, wholesome foods.

'Rab' Butler, Minister for Education, dismissed the study, exclaiming

> children are human and they run about too much, so they don't put on weight. School discipline always has this effect.

Neither the study nor the analysis appeared to have been scientific, but the outcome was the closure of the Camp Schools and the end of the experiment.

114   *A village victory celebration and party at Singleton at the end of the First World War.*

Women's Land Army

At the outbreak of the Second World War the government accepted the offer of Lady Trudie Denman, Honorary Director of the Women's Land Army (WLA), to transfer its headquarters out of London to her Balcombe Place home. The government was dilatory and only responded when she delivered an ultimatum, HQ or evacuees? The organisation was administered from this country base until 1943, when the growth in the WLA, from nothing in 1939 to 65,000, outgrew the premises and the organisation returned to London.

The original establishment of 35 administrators had to be supplemented as the service expanded. The lack of billets in Balcombe village meant commuting to work and the staff being transported from the station in the estate van, which made four return journeys daily. No additional petrol coupons were available, which put a severe strain on Lady Denman's generosity and contributed to the decision to revert to London.

115   *A 17-year-old Land Army girl in uniform.*

Lady Denman's contacts as the first National Chairman of the Women's Institutes (1916-46) and first President of the Family Planning Association (1933) gave her direct access to government and royalty. Correspondence with Kensington Palace revealed Queen Mary and Princess Alice's anxiety over the future of Brantridge Park in the event of Princess Beatrice dying. They were concerned it would become the victim of 'rude soldiering' and sought Lady Denman's cooperation to requisition it for the WLA, thereby averting such a fate.

Lady Denman overcame innumerable difficulties in driving the WLA forward, from lack of uniforms, caused by shortages of cloth and clothes coupons, and wages which were set at 32s. a week and 28s. for the 17-year-old recruits, to persuading employers to provide accommodation. The country was divided into regions, invariably overseen by a member of the aristocracy, thereby delivering a coherent policy through a series of regional conferences.

The reminiscences of the 'land girls' give a vivid insight into their wartime roles. Daphne Byrne spent the latter

116 *Lady Denman, Honorary Director of the Women's Land Army, presenting awards to Land Army girls at a county rally at Arundel Castle, 10 May 1943.*

years of the war at Lake Lane Nurseries, Barnham growing tomatoes and cucumbers in long glasshouses. Mr Barrett also grew chrysanthemums destined for Covent Garden, illegally, but it was worth him paying the subsequent fine. They were assisted by German and Italian prisoners of war. The former were hard working, apparently, but the Italians spent too much time combing their hair and admiring themselves in every available reflective surface. Indeed, one Italian POW chased Mrs Barrett around her kitchen with a carving knife when she called him 'a good for nothing' on account of his idleness. Others wanted to learn to milk but 'preferred to begin with a calf'.

There were respites from the daily chores. The Saturday night 'hops' in the nearby Officers Mess at Ford and Tangmere were sweaty affairs, dancing the night away in the arms of 'inexpert and painfully shy swains' to Glenn Miller and Victor Sylvester, courtesy of a wind-up gramophone. Daphne recalls how, in the absence of roll-on deodorants, the Land Girls used to sew preservers in their only dress to absorb the sweat and drown themselves with a 6d. bottle of 'Evening in Paris' perfume from Woolworths to counter the 'body odours' released by close encounters of a perspiring kind. To have had a 'good night kiss' was a daring experience. Other 'land girls' remember village events such as Barn Dances and Harvest Homes in Trotton Village Hall, where they became the 'belles of the ball' and were accorded 'three cheers'.

117 *The Farewell and Passing Out Parade of the Women's Land Army at Arundel Castle, 1950.*

Contrary to popular imagination, the 'land girls' claim they had neither the time nor opportunity to 'romp in the hay'. Judging from this letter, however, Headquarters seems to have shared in the popular misconception:

Good Night(s) Ladies

The Land Army relies less on rules for the conduct of its members than on common sense. There are exceptions and complaints have been received from several counties that some volunteers indulge in so many and such very late nights that their work, health and landladies suffer.

Parties are good fun and life would be dull without them but in wartime at least we ought to earn the right to have a party, and they should be limited to Saturdays and holidays. Work must come first.

The work of the Land Army is such that we cannot afford to leave any of it undone – unless we want the war to go on until we are too old to enjoy parties anyway!

The 'land girls' were only allocated one uniform to wear in all weathers. They found them warm in winter and cool in summer; the greatcoats were 'great' but the hats were 'a joke'. They were also issued with tin helmets which were hardly ever worn. A circular on gumboots (wellingtons) spelt out that they had to last the whole winter, and would only last if good care was taken of them. They should be worn only when absolutely necessary since when they wore out there would be no more. The circular added, 'You have been warned'; and the boots weren't even waterproof!

Lady Denman fought to have the Women's Land Army treated on the same terms as the armed forces but was prepared to make concessions on the materials as long as she could get the items. Baths were taken in tin tubs in front of the fire with a hose laid on from a copper in the kitchen to provide the hot water. After a day in the fields or glasshouses they were 'the best baths of a lifetime'.

The Farewell Parade took place on 21 October 1950 prior to the WLA being disbanded in November. Over 200,000 women served during the 11-year period with nearly 80,000 at the peak in August 1943. The WLA was conceived two years before war broke out and came into being on 1 June 1939, but only recruited when war was declared. In retrospect, some of the advertising was 'risqué', as farmers were encouraged to 'Try a Land Girl'. Loudspeaker vans toured the countryside, a 'talkie' recruitment film featuring Lady Denman was shown in cinemas, and 'Good Service Badges' (half diamonds for each six months' service) were awarded as incentives to maintain morale.

Lady Denman resigned on principle in 1945 after the WLA was excluded from post-war resettlement benefits, which was the final rejection of her campaign to have it recognised as the equal of the armed forces and civil defence. The Women's Land Army played an important role in feeding the country, and its contribution was respected and valued. It was a colourful interlude.

The Guinea Pig Club

The development of a unique organisation from a meeting of the 'Few' on 19 July 1941 over a bottle of sherry is one of the heart-warming stories of the war:

> We'll put the burnt airmen in an uncomfortable wooden hut at the rear of Queen Victoria Cottage Hospital, East Grinstead. There they will create an amazing spirit reminiscent of the spirit of a fighter squadron.
>
> When we receive more burnt airmen from heavy bombers whose morale will not be as high as the fighter crews who are the cream, the spirit will have wafted through the hospital and everybody will get better much quicker. Some may even return to use the killing skills in which the nation invested so much time and money. (Those that did carried a card inscribed 'in case of further trouble deliver the bits to Ward III, East Grinstead'.)
>
> To assist a speedy recovery for the chaps we'll recruit the prettiest nurses and put a fellow called McIndoe in charge of the lot because he not only seems capable at carving people up but also understanding their minds, which is every bit as important when dealing with burns cases.
>
> One more important point. We must have a matron who is a thoroughly good sort. She must welcome beer barrels in the wards and ignore her patients returning from London night-clubs in time for breakfast. The cottage hospital is entirely suitable. Matron Hall is a gem with a talent for turning a blind eye.

118 Guinea Pig *pub sign, East Grinstead.*

119 *Sir Archibald McIndoe and patients around the piano at an annual reunion.*

Anaesthesia for plastic surgery is a specialised branch of medicine and like Mr McIndoe they must be humanitarians. Our team is very special. Finally East Grinstead is a good, healthy spot convenient for London flesh pots to keep the chaps cheered up. The scented pinewoods contain healing properties particularly pertinent for guinea pigs. They also enclose the homes of some of the nation's wealthiest people which can't be bad for the chaps once they are on crutches. A club. That's the top priority.

It was this indomitable spirit which averted the threat of severely disabled, disfigured and mutilated men being tucked away in a quiet corner in the country out of sight and mind. The combined efforts of the patients, the skill and dedication of the staff, and the caring and supportive public of East Grinstead ensured that the horrors of war were not hidden but open to public gaze.

The heavily bandaged fliers recovering from their hangovers on that Sunday morning in 1941 had enjoyed their 'grogging party' so much that they resolved to form a grogging club to have regular meetings and reunions. A meeting was convened and minutes taken. There were to be three categories of membership:

1. The Guinea Pigs (patients)
2. The Scientists (staff)
3. The Royal Society for the Prevention of Cruelty to Guinea Pigs (friends and benefactors whose interest in the hospital and patients make the life of a Guinea Pig such a happy one).

Their humour in the face of adversity is captured in the Guinea Pig Anthem.

We are McIndoe's army
We are his Guinea Pigs,
With dermatomes and pedicles,
Glass eyes, false teeth and wigs.
And when we get our discharge
We'll shout with all our might:
'Per Ardua ad Astra',
We'd rather drink than fight.

John Hunter runs the gas works,
Ross Tilley wields the knife,
And if they are not careful
They'll have your flaming life.
So, Guinea Pigs, stand steady
For all your surgeons' calls
And if their hands aren't steady
They'll whip off both your ... ears.

We've had some mad Australians,
Some French, some Czechs, some Poles.
We've even had some Yankees,

God bless their precious souls.
While as for the Canadians
Ah! That's a different thing.
They couldn't stand our accent
And built a separate Wing.

We are McIndoe's army (repeat first verse)

The conjunction of a famous plastic surgeon, Sir
Archibald McIndoe ('The Boss' or 'The Maestro'), a
dedicated supporting cast of fellow surgeons, anaesthetists,
nurses and ancillary staff, and a very special succession
of 'gutsy' young men turned what could have been a
depressing, self-pitying, morale-sapping experience into
a joyful, supportive, morale-boosting one which carved
permanent friendships out of the depths of despair in
the midst of war. Those who recovered went on to live
full lives in the same way that a badly burned Simon
Weston re-built his life and became the image of the
spirit of the Falklands War. As one of the Guinea Pigs
wrote in the post-war years, 'I am up to my new eyelids
in work'!

South Harting War Memorial

On 29 June 1920 the Parochial Church Council of the parish of South
Harting applied to the Diocese of Chichester for a 'Faculty' to erect a War
Memorial to those who lost their lives in the First World War. It was to take
the form of a 22ft. high cross positioned in the churchyard between the
vestry and the main pathway. The Council commissioned the acclaimed
sculptor, Eric Gill, to carve the patron saints of England, Scotland, Wales
and Ireland around the base of the pedestal and an inscription on the face. It cost £250, raised by public subscription, and it was dedicated on 3 July 1921.

Eric Gill considered the Memorial to be an 'Illustra-
tion'. It was a 'stone carving' rather than a sculpture
exhibited at the Royal Academy, and should be judged
on that basis. 'The critics may not find beauty in it – but
they might as well try and fail as fail by not trying. Gill
argued that 'Beauty is neither a matter of "likeness of
nature" nor of "sentimental expressiveness" '.

Neville Duke

On 7 September 1953 Squadron Leader Neville Duke
broke the World Air Speed Record in a Hawker Hunter
WB188 powered by a Rolls-Royce 'Avon' engine off the

120 *South Harting War Memorial, carved by the eminent sculptor and artist Eric Gill in 1921.*
121 *Detail of St Andrew, fisher of men, from the base of the War Memorial in South Harting churchyard.*

122 Neville Duke, Bill Waterton and Teddy Donaldson at RAF Tangmere, the three test pilots of the High Speed Flight team.

coast of West Sussex, reaching a speed of 727.63 m.p.h. The attempt formed part of the flight development programme for the RAF being conducted by Hawkers, for whom Duke was the chief test pilot. Flying from the Hawker aerodrome at Dunsfold towards Chichester in 1951, he broke through the 'sound barrier' for the first time over Balls Cross near Petworth with an almighty 'queer bang' as a local put it to him. The village policeman recounted at *The Stag* how 'one moment all the chooks were there and next moment they wasn't. They were all blown up in one corner without feathers and me on my back in the middle of the fowl run'.

It was the final record under the original FAI regulations which required the attempt to be timed as the best of four consecutive runs over a measured three-kilometre course below 100 metres (effectively at sea level). The course 1,000 yards off Littlehampton was selected because weather records showed that attempts could be made on 22 of the 48 days between 1 August and 18 September, the best ratio in the country.

The record was orchestrated from RAF Tangmere, where Duke had been a member of the High Speed Flight team just after the end of the Second World War. He had a distinguished war record, ending as eighth-ranked combat fighter, registering 28 'kills' and earning himself a DFC, OBE, DSO (and two bars). On 7 September 1953 he took off from and landed at Tangmere after his successful record attempt between Shoreham and Bognor Regis, reaching maximum speed at 90 feet above the sea off Littlehampton. The next day he demonstrated the Hunter at the Farnborough Air Show and the following day had lunch with the Prime Minister at Chequers; an exhilarating weekend in more ways than one.

Six

LEISURE AND PLEASURE

Leisure pursuits have tended to reflect the times in which they were enjoyed, tranquil, peaceful periods spawning gentle sports such as bowls and cricket. Some sports, such as croquet, horse racing, hunting and shooting, have been associated with the 'upper classes', while others, such as soccer, with the 'working classes', and some such as stoolball with both. Similarly, some entertainments attract more spectators than participants and *vice versa*. At various times, specific activities have come into and then gone out of fashion. Today white-knuckle rides are popular while in the past menageries and zoos had their day, as did travelling fairs with their 'freaks'. West Sussex has experienced many of these trends.

'Bowles'

'Bowles' is known to have been played in the 14th century. It was banned by Edward II in 1361 because it had become so popular that it was interfering with archery practice. As late as 1541 'commoners' were forbidden to play and public bowling greens prohibited. It was the preserve of the middle and upper classes as only those owning land valued in excess of £100 could play on their own property. Playing bowls was a social occasion when invited guests 'drank tea'.

The earliest form of the game involved a straight path to a cone-shaped target but the introduction of bias in the 16th century revolutionised the game. By the 17th century bowls had become the 'national game', incorporating all classes. There was a bowling green in the Bishop's Palace gardens in Chichester, where people played for 'a stipulated sum per game or rubber'. Betting on the result of

123 *A gentle game of 'bowles' in the early 17th century, the centrepiece of social occasions in stately homes such as Petworth House, where a bowling green was shown on Tresswell's map of 1610.*

124 *The statue of a lioness at High Wood, Goodwood marking the site of the former menagerie.*

games was rife. In 1625 a bowling green was described as a place

> where three things are thrown away, besides the bowls viz. Time, Money and Curses; here men will wrangle for a hair's breadth and make a stir, where a straw would end the controversie.

Bowls was being played in Chichester at least as early as 1575, when John Gryorye was brought before the Church Court because:

> he often absented himself from divine service in the cathedral, and frequented bowling in public, sometimes in time of divine service.

St Mary's Hospital had 'a parcel of ye sayd farm called St Maries commonly used as a bowling green' where Little London stands today. In Westbourne, in 1623, six parishioners played bowls instead of going to church; they were each fined 10s., a substantial sum, and forced to do penance in the parish church. In Fittleworth in 1626 the same happened. Each confessed

> Whereas I did recently prophane the lord's holy sabboth by playing at Bowles with others of my neighbours in tyme of evening prayers, I am now most hartily sorry, And doe faythfully promise not to offend agayne in the like manner and to be more careful in coming to divine service and sanctifying the sabboth day.

'A Woman Tygerr'

> Now about this time [1725] was brought to Goodwood the novelty of many wild beasts, birds and other animals, and there kept in dens with iron gates made for them to be seen through, which drew a great number of people thither to see them, for in those days such a sight was rare indeed.

The 2nd Duke of Richmond had exploited his contacts and collected a remarkable menagerie of animals from all over the world for public view, 'a wondrous and costly hobby'. It was situated in the pleasure grounds, known as the High Wood, on the Goodwood Estate. The animals were housed in 'stone cells under ground and dark recesses – or passages – subturane'. The larger animals were kept in iron cages (making and transporting a 15ft. square cage to Goodwood cost £93 in 1726) and the smaller ones in collars and chains.

The menagerie attracted so many tourists that the Duke's steward informed him 'we are very much troubled with Rude Company to see the animals. Sunday last we had 4 or 5 hundred good and bad but I Can't say which was ye gretest number'. The experiment was not unique as Lady Egremont had a menagerie at Petworth and Sir Matthew Fetherstonhaugh another at Uppark, but the Goodwood version was larger and more ambitious. Safari parks at stately homes go back a long way.

The list of the Duke's 'pets' and their diet indicates the range of the beasts and the expense involved in keeping them.

	Pounds a Day	
	Horse	Beef
5 Woulves	10	10
2 Tygerrs	4	4
1 Lyon	3	3
3 lepers (leopards?)	4	4
1 Sived Cat	1	1
A Tyger Cat	1	1
A Jack All	½	½
3 Vulters 2 Eagles	5	5
1 Kite	1	1
2 Owls	1	1
That is all yt Eat Flesh	70lbs.	
3 bears	2 loafs	
1 Large Monkey	¼ loaf	
A Woman Tygerr	1 loaf	
3 Racoons	¼ loaf	
3 Small Monkeys	¼ loaf	
Armadilla/ 1 pecaverre	¼ loaf	
7 Caseawarris	½ loaf	
That is all ye annimalls that eat Bread		

The list does not tell the whole story. Cereals, vegetables, fruit, straw and chickens supplemented the basic diet of flesh and bread, while the eagles fed on sheeps 'heads and bullocks' hearts.

The 2nd Duke died on 8 August 1750 and his menagerie died with him. It had been declining for many years. The cost of keeping the animals was very expensive and they were not being fed regularly because they 'must be obliged to faste some days in ye week but what days I can't say'. Correspondence reveals a continuous series of deaths brought on by unsuitable conditions, food and temperature.

The sole reminder of this exotic and eclectic collection is the recumbent statue of the 'Lyon', or lioness, which the Duke erected in her memory when she died within a few months of her arrival. The identity of the 'Woman Tygerr' remains a mystery but no doubt her presence added to the mystique, and attendance, at the menagerie.

125 *Dovecotes, as here at Parham Park, often containing more than 1,000 nesting boxes, provided sport as well as a culinary delicacy.*

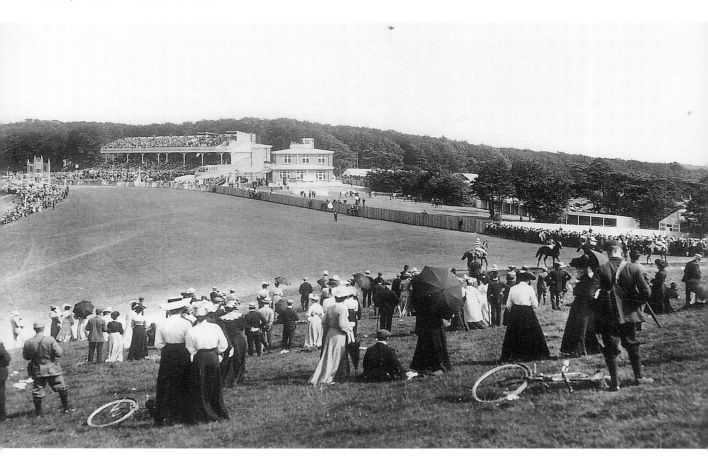

126 *Goodwood racecourse in 1903, when it celebrated the centenary of the 'Annual Meeting'.*

Glorious Goodwood

The construction of Goodwood racecourse began in 1800 and the first race took place in April 1802. In the following year 'The Annual [as it then was] Meeting' was moved to the end of July, where it has remained ever since. Part of the original horseshoe-shaped track has been incorporated into the present course. An editorial in the local newspaper in May 1802 addressed the Duke in the most deferential terms:

> To the efforts of equestrian skill is to be added the princely and almost unprecedented munificence of the noble founder of the Goodwood Races, in providing the new-erected stand with a collation which might be entitled a refrigarium, for the access was as easy as the reception was elegant and hospitable. The thanks of the county in general, and of this city (Chichester) and its vicinity in general are largely due to His Grace the Duke of Richmond for having thus munificently and liberally instituted an establishment of most material local benefit both as a source of pecuniary advantage to the inhabitants and as a means of forwarding to notice and increasing the consequence of the western part of the county. We can only add our wish that the illustrious founder may for years enjoy in health and happiness this promising scion, planted by his own hand, a wish in which we shall be joined by all true Sussex patriots.

The 'Sport of Kings' was a pastime frequented and enjoyed by the nobility and gentry and supported by the tenants and inhabitants of the local neighbourhood. As transport improved, especially after the railway arrived in 1844, the clientele altered. The races attracted 'foul mouthed cabmen, filthy touts, lynx eyed thieves and bloated bullies', and there was talk of two meetings a year, 'God forbid'. All lodgings and beds within a 15-mile radius were in a state of great siege, and there was a general anticipation of a 'great harvest'.

127 *The Royal Box, Goodwood in 1903 with Edward VII, who considered Goodwood the close of the London social season before sailing at Cowes and shooting in Scotland.*

Racegoers complained that Chichester's inhabitants were 'Shylocks', and that 'The Swan' should be renamed 'The Shark'.

The 3rd Duke was advised by Lord George Bentinck and the partnership turned Goodwood into the 'model' for other courses and race meetings. It was 'without rival', 'near perfection', 'beautifully staged', 'efficiently organised', offering 'good prize money', 'the prettiest ladies in England', 'the prettiest peasantry in the country', 'a most magnificent race meeting', and 'a paradise combining everything that is enjoyable in life'. It was a giant garden party and 'more like a State Opening of Parliament'.

The Duke and Bentinck also became leading owners and employed John Kent as the successful trainer who turned the stable into the best in the country. The partnership disbanded in 1845 when Bentinck decided to give up racing and enter politics. He sold 'Surplice', which then won the Derby and St Leger, and in consoling him Disraeli coined the phrase 'the Blue Riband of the Turf'.

Bare-knuckle Prizefighting on Crawley Down

In the early 1970s the *Prizefighters* public house in Crawley Down, between East Grinstead and Crawley, was renamed the *Royal Oak*. The name marked the period in the first half of the 19th century when the rectangle of common land where the village of Crawley Down developed half a century later was the most celebrated prizefighting venue in the country.

The sport of prizefighting grew throughout the second half of the 18th century, largely as a consequence of its being made illegal in 1750. By 1800 it had a following drawn from all levels of society. The excitement of illegality allied to betting on the bouts attracted thousands, and 'if the carriages had all been placed in one line they would have stretched from London to Crawley'. In 1821 over £200,000 was wagered on one fight. Venues were

128 *A prize fight between Randall and Martin on Crawley Down in 1819 epitomised the rituals inseparable from the ring. The top-hatted seconds and bottle holders, pictured, are not 'gentlemen' but fighters Tom Oliver, Tom Jones and Ben Burn dressed up for the occasion.*

kept secret until a day or so before the fight and communicated to devotees, much as raves are today.

Crawley Down was a particular favourite of wealthy clientele, being roughly half way between London and Brighton. They rated prizefighting on a par with bear baiting, cock fighting and horse racing. The poorer classes regarded the fights as light relief from arduous toil and more as a spectacle than a gambling opportunity. Prizefighting had a language of its own which preserved its mystique amongst the 'fancy' (followers) who witnessed the 'mill' (fight). The gentlemen spectators were 'amateurs' and the participants were 'pugilists'. Both groups were 'milling around' the arena. In the absence of photographs, these labels were devised and exploited by sports journalists to convey the colour and atmosphere of the occasion.

The boxers were also given 'nicknames' to cultivate their 'image' and identify their, usually humble, origins. Jack Martin, a baker, was styled 'The Master of the Rolls', Tom Hickman was advertised as 'The Gas Man', Ned Turner was an 'Out and Outer', while peerless Jack Randall was 'The Nonpareil', although he failed to depose Tom Cribb as Champion of England.

The tactics employed were more akin to all-in wrestling than Marquess of Queensberry rules, and included the notorious 'Suit in Chancery' or 'Half Nelson', where the head was immobilised by one arm and the face pummelled with the other. One report eulogised the manner in which Jack

Cooper won 'with his left hand only'; another related how:

> On Thursday last a boxing match took place at Crawley Down between John Smith and Ned Stanford, two professional pugilists. After a severe conflict which betrayed more of a savage encounter than a scientific display of the gymnastic art, it terminated in favour of Smith, Stanford having given in while still breathing and standing on his legs, much to the disappointment of the knowing ones.

Spectators usually had their money's worth because fights lasted a long time, although they could be ended abruptly because of the appearance of the law. The fighters challenged each other by 'throwing their hats in the ring'. There was no defined length to a fight and the round finished when one of the boxers was knocked down; a fight only finished when one of the contestants 'threw in the towel' or collapsed with sheer exhaustion. The fight in Chichester in 1824 between the English champion, Tom Spring, and John Langan, his Irish challenger for the title and a £500 prize, lasted 77 rounds and took 1 hour 55 minutes before Spring was declared winner because Fagan was 'insensible'. Frequently a superior fighter stretched the fight out to give the spectators value for money, and bribery was not uncommon.

129   *Tom Sayer, English bare-knuckle boxing champion, who lived at Waterfall Cottage, Sullington. He lost a 'world' championship bout to 'Benicia Boy' (USA) after 42 rounds, having injured his right hand in round four. He died in 1865 at the age of 39 years.*

Prizefighting brought trade and money to Crawley Down and places along the routes. The conditions of the Sussex roads made overnight stops essential, to the benefit of inns and private dwellings whose occupants 'were prepared to sit up all night if they could turn their beds to good account asking only 15s. or £1 for a night's sleep'. The 'swells' and the 'brilliant' aimed to do the round trip in a day, although the buggies and barouches left stranded told another story.

The ring in Crawley Down was reputed to have been in an 'amphitheatre' protecting the crowd from prying eyes and accentuating the illicit feeling. Sometimes there was a 'ring' or 'stage' but more often the fights took place at ground level with a circle of wagons holding the crowds back. Hailsham, Copthorne Common, Blindley Heath and Lowfield Heath were other local prizefighting venues, but none attained the status and fame of Crawley Down, which for five brief years between 1819-23 was pre-eminent in England.

The Cradle of Cricket

West Sussex has been dubbed 'the cradle of cricket'. The earliest reference is found in the annual presentments of the churchwardens at Boxgrove to the Bishop in 1622 and mentions: 'Five (named) men with others whose

130 *Princess Alexandra laying the foundation stone of Chichester Festival Theatre on 12 May 1961 and converting 'The Impossible Theatre' (the title of a book written by the inspiration behind the project, Leslie Evershed-Martin) into reality.*

131 *The front cover of a programme for a fund raising cricket match for the Sackville College, East Grinstead in September 1955, which attracted a crowd of over 4,000 despite inclement weather.*

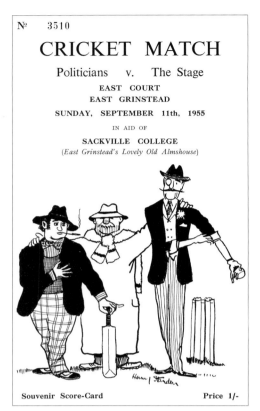

name I have no notion of for playing cricket in the churchyard during Divine Service on Sunday fifth of May after sufficient warnings to the contrary'. They broke the church windows with the ball and there was a danger of the children 'having their braynes beaten out'.

The Duke of Richmond was an enthusiastic supporter, player and gambler. In 1727 his team played at Peper Harrow, near Godalming, where the laws of cricket were first formulated to avoid a dispute over a wager of £1,000. He sponsored the Slindon team, virtually all of whom represented England v. Kent in 1744. The star batsman was Richard Newland, a Chichester surgeon whose nephew, Richard Nyren, another team member, went to keep the *Bat and Ball* at Broad Halfpenny Down and by so doing ensured that Hambledon rather than Slindon became synonymous with the game.

The Greatest Batsman Ever?

The accolade of being the greatest batsman ever was accorded to Kumar Shri Ranjitsinhji, 'Ranji', in 1907. Until this time it had been accepted that the honour belonged to the legendary W.G. Grace, and now it would be attributed to Don Bradman.

POLITICIANS		THE STAGE	
EARL DE LA WARR (*Captain*) (PATRON OF SACKVILLE COLLEGE)		MR. JOHN MILLS (*Captain*)	
VISCOUNT KILMUIR		MR. RICHARD ATTENBOROUGH	
MAJOR GWILYM LLOYD GEORGE		MR. DOUGLAS FAIRBANKS	
MR. HAROLD MACMILLAN		MR. LEO GENN	
SIR WALTER MONCKTON		MR. REX HARRISON	
THE EARL OF SELKIRK		MR. RICHARD HEARNE ("MR. PASTRY")	
VISCOUNT GAGE		MR. DAVID NIVEN	
LORD HAWKE		MR. JOHN SLATER	
LT.-COL. BROMLEY-DAVENPORT		MR. JOHN UNDERDOWN	
MR. G. H. G. DOGGART (SUSSEX C.C.C.)		MR. DENIS COMPTON (ENGLAND AND MIDDLESEX C.C.C.)	
MR. G. L. COGGER (SUSSEX C.C.C.)		MR. J. J. WARR (MIDDLESEX C.C.C.)	
	TOTAL ...		*TOTAL ...*

Umpires : SIR HARRY SINDERSON PASHA
(WARDEN OF SACKVILLE COLLEGE)
MR. S. G. POWER
(CAPTAIN, EAST GRINSTEAD C.C.)
COMMENTARY BY MR. JOHN SNAGGE

Scorers : MR. P. F. C. HOBDEN
(EAST GRINSTEAD C.C.)
MR. J. E. LAWRENCE
(EAST GRINSTEAD C.C.)

Competition Prizes : AN AUTOGRAPHED BAT (both Teams), Two MINIATURE BATS (with Autographs of Politicians and The Stage respectively), a BOTTLE OF CHAMPAGNE, a BOTTLE OF WHISKY, a BOTTLE OF SHERRY, an ELECTRIC IRON, THEATRE TICKETS, DUNHILL LIGHTER, and a TELEVISION SET.
A BOTTLE OF GIN will be awarded to the holder of the Score-Card Lucky Number.

132 *The star-studded teams in the Politicians v. Stage cricket match at East Grinstead in 1955, many of whom subsequently became lords and knights of the realm. Richard, later Lord Richard, Attenborough had to be carried from the field bleeding profusely from a wound in his head when he completely misjudged a catch on the boundary and was felled like a log. He was taken to the Queen Victoria Hospital where Sir Archibald McIndoe sewed the wound with 12 stitches.*

Ranji burst on the cricketing scene in 1895 when, on his first appearance for Sussex, he scored 150 and 77 not out against an MCC team which included W.G. Grace, who bowled 'Ranji' in the first innings. In his first season he scored 1,766 runs at an average of 50.16 runs an innings, including four centuries. In his second season he exceeded expectations, scoring 2,113 runs at an average of 58.25 and eight centuries, and in 1899 was the first to score over 3,000 runs in a season. In his career, which finished in 1921, he scored over 25,000 runs at an average of 45.00 and for Sussex over 18,000 runs at an average of 63.24, including 14 double centuries.

Statistics do not tell the whole story. An Indian nobleman, 'Ranji' was dark-skinned and elegant, a magician with a flowing synchronised movement of body and bat which was accentuated by his habit of wearing a rippling silk shirt buttoned at the wrists. He was a graceful batsman with the ability to stroke the ball all over the pitch. The famous cricket commentator Neville Cardus described 'Ranji' in these terms:

> When he turned approved science upside down and changed the geometry of batting to an esoteric legerdemain we were bewitched to the realms of rope dancers and snake charmers; this was cricket of oriental sorcery, glowing with a dark beauty of its own, a beauty with its own mysterious axis and balance.

133   Ranjitsinhji and friends finishing a meal at Goring in 1907 before a hunting party.

134   Gatwick racecourse and aerodrome in 1936 when it was the headquarters of a flying club.

His Highness the Jam Sahib of Nawangar returned to India to assume the rule of his State but left behind a cricketing legacy. He was a most hospitable man, especially noted for the big game hunting parties which ultimately shortened his career after he lost an eye in a shooting accident. On one occasion he entertained teams to a shooting party at Shillinglee, near Fernhurst, who had failed to turn up to play their opponents at Chichester, assuming that because it was raining in Fernhurst it was also raining in Chichester! It was a bitter disappointment to the huge crowd that had gathered to watch his majestic batting.

Gatwick – Racecourse to Runway

Gatwick Airport opened in 1931 as a private aerodrome comprising a grass runway, hangar and petrol pump. It was popular with the Surrey Aero Club and used by those attending horse racing meetings at Gatwick racecourse, which opened in 1891. The last meeting was held in 1947. During the First World War it hosted the Grand National and the 1918 winner, Poethlyn, was ridden by Ernie Piggott, Lester Piggott's grandfather. Commercial flying began in 1936 after BOAC improved facilities, including draining the often waterlogged runway. The airport was used by the RAF in the Second World War for reconnaissance and photography.

After a hiatus at the end of the war the government took the decision to develop and expand facilities and Gatwick was re-opened by HM The Queen in 1958. At the time it was state-of-the-art with integrated road, rail and air connections. It became part of and the largest employer in Crawley New Town, which was designated one of eight New Towns to relieve London in 1947.

Stoolball, the Quintessential Sussex Game

The origins of stoolball are vague but there are references in the late medieval period to clergy fulminating against a similar game being played by both the gentry and the 'rascality' in churchyards on Sundays and disturbing services.

> Stool Ball is a game shrouded in mystery. Some descriptions of the game are indeed so hazy as to put it beyond the understanding of all but a select few. (John Lowerson, *Sussex Archaeological Collections*, 133 (1995), p.265)

Stoolball was a summer game promoted by the clergy, gentry and country houses to integrate villagers, build a community spirit and curb the exuberance of youth. It was played by their 'genteel' daughters abetted by a few 'strapping' village girls to inject the necessary strength and 'rusticity'. It was always considered a female pursuit.

Two wickets, boards one foot square mounted on poles 4ft. 6 inches tall, placed 16 yards apart and usually free standing, constituted the 'pitch'. Two teams of 11-a-side used willow bats 7½ inches across and shaped like table tennis bats to hit a soft ball as far as possible and accumulate runs. The side scoring the most runs won the game. Often played on the outfields of cricket grounds, the game broke links with cricket in the Victorian period when the latter became 'commercialised', charging admission to watch matches. Stoolball retained the purity and essence of the countryside and became freely open to players of any age, sex, class and experience.

It was a highly localised phenomenon, particularly popular in the Wealden villages where rules were passed on by oral tradition, and often exhibited subtle differences between adjacent villages. The first codification of rules published in 1867 was intended to prevent squabbles over local interpretations. The Sussex 'clean catch' rule is unique. Competition was limited to walking distances between villages or daylight travel by farm wagons.

Just for once a 'traditional' game has thrown up both a hero and villain. 'Major' W.W. Grantham, an 'eccentric' West Sussex lawyer and landowner,

135 *W.W. Grantham was a contradictory character who attempted to popularise stoolball on his extensive travels around the world, promoting it as a sophisticated 'middle-class' game but dressing himself and his Sussex Downsmen team in beaver hats and Sussex smocks at home to advertise the game's village origins.*

136 *(Above) A stoolball game at Horsham Park in the 1870s portrayed as a 'Fête Champêtre', with carriage-borne families watching the players in between socialising in a marquee.*

137 *(Left) W.W. Grantham introduces the wife of a Japanese diplomat to the stoolball bat.*

138 *(Right) L. Farley in his 'cycling gear' with his 'Penny farthing', the catalyst for the boom in the formation of cycling clubs in the last quarter of the 19th century.*

139 *The winner of the Littlehampton-Arundel 'Hod' race, Easter 1920. Each competitor carried a hod of bricks seven miles each way.*

140 *Bathing machines on the beach at Bognor in the 1890s.*

141 *Portfield Bonfire Society loading their home-made torches onto carts to illuminate the annual 'Guy Fawkes' procession. An Act of 1605 gave thanks for deliverance from Papist oppression and ordered that the day be observed for ever but, in fact, most Bonfire Societies are relatively recent revivals.*

142 *Donkeys on the beach at Littlehampton in the 1890s, a traditional seaside attraction.*

attempted to use his contacts, muscle and organising skills to develop stoolball as a mass activity, portraying it as masculine and military. By lobbying and twisting influential arms he arranged a demonstration match at Lords in 1917, an arrangement which continued for a further 10 years, and for 20 more years in the gardens of Buckingham Palace, which were kindly loaned by King George V. His trump card was promoting its rôle in convalescence after the First World War. In 1923 he formed the Stoolball Association of Great Britain, advertising the game as a cheap sport, easy to learn, to be played and enjoyed by all abilities, thus contributing to the physical and mental health of the nation and developing that 'indefinable' team spirit.

He spoke on the radio, made promotional films, broadcast on the embryonic television service from Alexandra Palace, and travelled the world publicising stoolball with evangelistic fervour. Yet at home he was so committed to the rural origins of the game that his Sussex Downsmen team dressed in black linen Sussex smocks, redolent of labourers and shepherds, with beaver hats, and travelled to games thus attired in order to attract attention and publicity.

At the end of the First World War a furious row broke out when the Sussex Matriarchs, led by the recently founded Women's Institutes, determined to resist Grantham's takeover bid and restore female control. They established women's leagues throughout the county and formed the Sussex Federation. The rivalry continued until the outbreak of the Second World War, both organisations running in parallel. Grantham died in 1942 and with him the national body. The purists still insist on women-only teams while the realists advocate mixed teams to ensure the survival of the ancient Sussex game of stoolball.

Frederick Henry Royce

143 *Frederick Henry Royce at the gate of his house in West Wittering.*

Frederick Henry Royce lived at West Wittering from 1917-33 after he retired on account of the ill health which dogged him throughout his life. At 10 years of age he was a newspaper boy with W. H. Smith and he only received 1½ years of elementary education. But he was studious and blessed with a genius for designing aero and car engines.

Despite the prediction he had only a month to live, he produced some of his finest achievements during his retirement. In 1919 Alcock and Brown flew the Atlantic for the first time using one of his 'Eagle' engines. Congratulations arrived by telegraph. 'Isn't this a wonderful day for West Wittering? The man who designed Alcock and Brown's engine lives here,' a telegraph boy was asked. 'I wish they hadn't done it on a Sunday as I have already had to cycle six times from Birdham', he replied. The congratulations were repeated when Sir Ross Smith and his son made the first flight to Australia.

Royce was a workaholic who established an 'elite' team of designers and draughtsmen in a workshop at West Wittering in his 'ceaseless quest for perfection'. He is credited with the first six-cylinder cars and the Rolls-Royce 'Phantom', as well as the Falcon, Hawk, Condor and Merlin engines. The last Schneider trophy for seaplanes in 1931 was won by his Rolls-Royce 'R' engine over a course in the Solent which had its apex at West Wittering as a tribute to him. He was too ill to witness the race but choirboys sang 'For he's a jolly good fellow' outside his curtained windows. The opening of the BMW Rolls-Royce factory at nearby Goodwood in 2003 is a reminder of the West Sussex association with the original firm.

INDEX

References which relate to illustrations are given in **bold**.